Applied Math Se

SOLVING
WORD PROBLEMS

BY STAN VERNOOY

COVER DESIGN BY KATHY KIFER

A Breath of Fresh Air

GarlicPress

To four women who changed my life:
Joan Roxberg
Dorothy Young
March Thompson
and
my wife, Anne Padgett

Published by:
Garlic Press
605 Powers St.
Eugene, OR 97402

ISBN 0-931993-80-6
Order Number GP-080

www.garlicpress.com

TABLE OF CONTENTS

Thousands (probably millions) of students have said about word problems, "It's only the setting up that I don't get. Once the equation is set up I know how to solve it." This book is intended for all of those students, and for their teachers, parents, and tutors.

This book intends to provide a consistent and logical approach to setting up word problems. There will be no special techniques, charts, or diagrams which apply to only one, narrowly defined, type of problem. Although there are discussions of several specific applications, the discussion of each application will be in the context of an overall strategy for solving *any* word problem.

There is a reason for approaching word problems as a broad, general skill instead of focusing on specific applications. The fact is, it is a rare day indeed that someone comes up to you and asks, "If Betty is 8 years older than her sister Jenny, and 19 years ago Betty was three times as old as Jenny was, then how old is Jenny?" If you learn to solve problems like that one (and problems in other strictly defined categories), then what have you learned? Perhaps you have learned how to get an A in your math course, but why are you taking math in the first place? Word problems are part of the mathematics curriculum for a good reason: They illustrate the connection between mathematics and clear, critical thinking on any subject. Word problems emphasize the precise definition of terms, the making of only those assertions which specifically apply to the issues or objects under discussion, and the application of careful reasoning in problem solving. These are all vital skills in any intellectually challenging profession, in forming thoughtful judgments about political and educational issues, and in making personal decisions.

This book is addressed to students and teachers of mathematics at all levels from beginning algebra through differential calculus. If you know how to solve linear equations for one variable, most of the book will be understandable to you.

The book contains almost no purely mathematical material. If you are studying or teaching algebra, the book assumes that you know how to solve equations or that you have access to that knowledge elsewhere. The same applies to the definitions of trigonometric functions if you are a trigonometry student, and to differentiation and finding the maximum or minimum point of a function if you are doing calculus. The Appendix contains many of the formulas and definitions which may be needed in solving word problems, but no explanations of the formulas are given—they are there only for reference.

Even if you are a calculus or trigonometry student, I *strongly* recommend that you read the entire book from the beginning instead of going straight to the chapters which deal specifically with trigonometry or calculus. Many trigonometry and calculus students have developed bad habits in their approach to word problems, and have gotten away with those bad habits because their native intelligence has enabled them to get the right answers despite their disorderly procedures. Suddenly, in calculus or trigonometry, their lack of a sound strategy for setting up word problems catches up with them. Reading this book from the beginning should help to cure that situation.

In addition to the exercises at the end of the chapters, the actual text is interspersed with exercises (the answers to which are in the back of the book) so that you may check your understanding of the material as you go along. DO NOT SKIP THESE EXERCISES! Without them, you may find yourself confused, for example, on page 41, not realizing that you lost the thread of the discussion back on page 19.

Two comments on the terminology in this book:

1. The phrases "story problems" and "word problems" mean the same thing.

2. The unidentified generic reader, teacher, or student may be either male or female. To avoid the awkwardness of constantly repeating phrases like "her/his" or "(s)he," I have assumed about half the time that the person in question is female, and about half the time that the person is male.

One final note: As a community college mathematics instructor, the author of this book has discovered that some students are going through their entire grade school and high school careers without being required to learn to do word problems. Even their teachers tell them that "story problems are just too hard," or that "nobody can do word problems," and skip over the material. It must be stated in the strongest possible terms that such a practice is doing a terrible disservice to the students. The fact is, solving word problems does **not** require a special talent beyond your capabilities. It probably does require more time than you and your teachers have traditionally devoted to the subject. But if you're willing to skip the next few episodes of your favorite TV show, you can find enough time (you can catch the missed episodes in the reruns anyway). Solving story problems, and indeed doing any mathematics, is only the *very careful* application of common sense. So if you've already decided that you can't possibly learn to do word problems, then please **change your mind**.

(Yes you can!)

COMMON SENSE

Before you do *anything*, read the problem! Then, before you do anything else, come up with a commonsense estimate of the answer. This process has two advantages:

1. If your answer is wildly different from your estimate, you'll know to go back and check your work.

2. The process of coming up with an estimate will make you familiar with what the problem really says, and what it really asks for.

EXAMPLES

○ *The area of a rectangle is 126 square inches, and the perimeter is 50 inches. What are the dimensions of the rectangle?*

APPLYING COMMON SENSE: One fact we can get immediately is that neither dimension (the length or the width) could possibly be more than 25 inches, because the perimeter includes two lengths and two widths. If we think about the problem a little more, we can get a ballpark figure by trying some combinations which would give us the right perimeter or the right area. For example, the dimensions 6×21 would give us the right area, and in that case the perimeter would be 54. Since 54 isn't all that far from the required 50, our guess of 6×21 probably isn't too far off. (The actual answer is 7×18.)

○ *Mary can paint the entire house in 30 hours, and Bob can paint it in 22 hours. How long will it take them to paint the house working together?*

APPLYING COMMON SENSE: Before you even put a mark on your paper, you must know that it won't take them 52 hours! If Mary can do it in 30 hours, how can it possibly take 52 hours when she has help? But we can get a good estimate (in fact, a remarkably close estimate) by reasoning as follows:

If Mary had the help of someone who was exactly as fast as she was, then that would cut her time in half. In other words, "two Marys" would require

15 hours. Similarly, if Bob had the help of someone who was exactly as fast as he was, it would cut his time in half, and so "two Bobs" would take 11 hours. Since we have one Bob and one Mary, the answer is almost certainly somewhere between 11 and 15, so we might guess 13 hours.

Having established this estimate, we would realize that we must have made a mistake somewhere if we came up with, for example, 1.5 hours or 483 hours.

○ *Tickets for a flight from Dallas to San Francisco are $363 for adults and $242 for children. A plane took off with a full load of 168 passengers, and the total ticket sales were $57,717. How many adults and how many children were aboard?*

APPLYING COMMON SENSE: At first glance, we can at least say that the numbers of adults and children will both be between 0 and 168. But in fact we can do better than that. Let's just calculate how much the total ticket sales would have been if we had an equal number of adults and children. In that case, the number of adults and the number of children would each be 84, and the total ticket sales would have been:

$$84(363) + 84(242) = 30,492 + 20,328 = 50,820$$

That number ($50,820) is less than what the ticket sales really were, which was $57,717. The only way the ticket sales could be more than $50,820 is if there were more than 84 adults and fewer than 84 children (because adults pay more than the children). Therefore, we can say for sure that our answer for the number of adults should be between 84 and 168, and the answer for the number of children should be between 0 and 84.

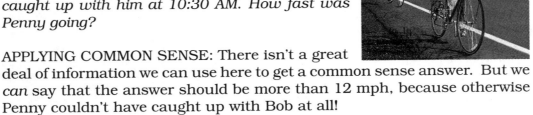

○ *Bob Gorkle left for a bicycle trip at 8:00 AM, cycling at 12 mph. Penny Jarkle followed Bob 30 minutes later, leaving from the same point, and caught up with him at 10:30 AM. How fast was Penny going?*

APPLYING COMMON SENSE: There isn't a great deal of information we can use here to get a common sense answer. But we *can* say that the answer should be more than 12 mph, because otherwise Penny couldn't have caught up with Bob at all!

The commonsense answers in the examples we have given may seem too obvious. But you would be surprised (maybe) at the number of students who confidently hand in a test paper stating that Penny was going $\frac{3}{8}$ of a mile per hour, or that there were 2,738 children on the flight in the previous problem.

Exercise

In all cases, just come up with a range of reasonable values for the answer. **Do NOT try to solve the problem.**

1. A car which originally sold for $24,000 is now selling for the reduced price of $22,000. What is the percent markdown?

2. A board 5 feet long is to be cut into three pieces; two pieces will be equal in length, and the third will be 6 inches shorter than the other two. How long will the two longer pieces be?

3. The sum of Sally's age and her daughter's age is 52. Sally was three times as old as her daughter four years ago. How old is Sally?

4. A car was driven 45 mph for 1.5 hours, and then increased in speed. After a total driving time of 3 hours, the car had traveled 145 miles. How fast was the car driven in the second half of the journey?

5. A purse full of dimes and nickels contains 75 coins worth $4.70. How many dimes and how many nickels are in the purse?

6. A businesswoman paid $69.47 to rent a car. The rental agreement provided for a charge of $39.50 plus 27¢ per mile driven. How far was the car driven?

7. A student took a test which included 35 multiple-choice questions, 10 true-false, and 5 short-answer questions. The student got 32 of the multiple-choice and 4 of the short-answer questions correct. He also got exactly 82% of all questions correct. How many true-false questions did he get correct?

8. LaDonna bought 324 ounces of soft drink. The soft drink came in 12-ounce, 16-ounce, and 32-ounce containers. She bought at least one of each size container. How many 16-ounce containers could she have bought? (Note: there isn't enough information to find exactly how many of each kind she bought. But there is enough information to come up with a reasonable range of answers.)

9. Ray and Letitia can rake the lawn in 50 minutes by working together. Letitia can rake it in 2 hours working alone. How long does it take Ray to do the job alone?

10. The smallest angle in a triangle is 40° smaller than the largest angle. How large is the largest angle? (Again, there is not enough information for an exact answer.)

DEFINING QUANTITIES

 ## About Defining Variables

When trying to do a word problem, many students make a mistake as soon as they put their first mark on the paper. Immediately, they try to set up an equation to solve. THAT IS THE WRONG THING TO DO!!! The right thing to do is to first define your variable(s)—in other words, write down each letter you are going to use in the problem, along with a clear and precise explanation of exactly what that letter stands for. You can't write an accurate equation involving the letter x unless you know exactly what x means. And if you can't write down a clear and precise explanation of what x means, then you don't know what it means!

If you are a comparatively advanced reader, in the habit of solving problems by immediately writing an equation and then solving it, you will object at this point. "I've been getting the answers right without doing this," you are saying. "Why should I change now?"

The response is that you can only go so far without learning the basic skill of defining variables. You are probably reading this book in the first place because you have reached a point in your mathematical progress where word problems are giving you trouble. By far, the most common reason that students have trouble with word problems is that they have only a fuzzy idea of what the letters in the equation(s) stand for. If you don't know exactly what x and y stand for, then it's very unlikely that you can set up correct equations involving x and y. This chapter of the book will cover the procedures and pitfalls of defining variables for story problems.

In this chapter, we will talk about how to identify the quantities in a word problem which need to be defined with a variable (letter) or with an algebraic expression (a combination of numbers and variables involving operations like addition, multiplication, etc.). At first, we will simply assign a separate letter to each unknown quantity. In a later chapter, we will talk about how to reduce the number of variables we use, by replacing some of the letters with algebraic expressions involving the others (for example, if quantity y is 1 less than quantity x, we can use x and $x - 1$ instead of x and y to describe the two quantities).

If you are a beginning or intermediate algebra student, you may find that a very few of the examples in this chapter are more complicated than you usually have to deal with. But, at least until you get to the chapters devoted specifically to trigonometry or calculus, try to do the exercises anyway. You don't have to know the mathematical procedures for solving complicated sets of equations, because this book doesn't deal with that. But you should be able to understand the ideas behind defining variables, even for those more advanced equations.

The Nastiest Word in Story Problem Solving

Suppose your class is discussing a particular word problem. At some point, a student might ask something like, "Isn't it $x + 2$?"

If your teacher is as ill-tempered as the author of this book, she will probably answer, "Isn't WHAT $x + 2$?"

When you are working with word problems, try with all your might to avoid using the word "it." Every time you find yourself saying, "It must be 43 times t," ask yourself, "What do I mean by 'it'?" If you find the question hard to answer, then you haven't thought the problem through! Most story problems involve more than one quantity, and "it" could mean any one of them. You can't talk accurately about a quantity unless you know exactly what quantity you're talking about!

Rules for Defining Variables

 RULE 1: "It" is the nastiest word in story problem solving.

 RULE 2: Each variable must stand for a *numeric* quantity.

EXAMPLE

Define the variables for this problem:

Mary is 7 years older than Jill. Two years ago, she was twice as old as Jill is now. How old are Mary and Jill?

SOLUTION:

We are not going to solve this problem just yet, but we are going to talk about the variables. The first thing a student might do wrong in this problem is to say:

M = Mary
J = Jill

This is wrong, because **Mary and Jill are not numbers**! They are people! (Or perhaps orangutans.) The variables M and J cannot stand for Mary and Jill! Now, don't say, "Aw, you know what I mean!" If you don't really mean that M stands for Mary, then don't say it! What you probably want to say is:

M = Mary's age
J = Jill's age

This is much better (although not perfect yet), because Mary's age and Jill's age are numeric quantities. Mary and Jill are not.

But why isn't it perfect? Because of the next rule.

 RULE 3: Each variable must stand for one and only one quantity.

EXAMPLE

Let's look again at the problem:

Mary is 7 years older than Jill. Two years ago, she was twice as old as Jill is now. How old are Mary and Jill?

SOLUTION:

Just a few minutes ago, we defined our variables as:

M = Mary's age
J = Jill's age

Now look again at the statement of the problem. Is there only one "Mary's age" in the problem? The answer is **no**. The first sentence of the problem talks about Mary's age **now**, and the second sentence talks about Mary's age **two years ago**. Those are not the same numbers! And we cannot use the letter M to stand for both! If M is going to stand for Mary's age now, then we need another variable (or maybe an expression involving M and/or J) to stand for Mary's age two years ago. [Note: Many readers will realize at this point that if we define M as Mary's age now, then we could define Mary's age two years ago as $M - 2$. But remember that in this section we are just assigning a separate variable to each unknown quantity. We will talk later about defining some quantities with algebraic expressions involving other quantities.] We need to understand this important fact: There are two "Mary's ages" in the problem. Therefore, we would be making a serious mistake if we allowed M to stand only for "Mary's age." What we should do is define our variables this way:

M = Mary's age now
N (or $M - 2$)= Mary's age two years ago
J = Jill's age now

[Note that we don't need a variable or an expression for Jill's age two years ago—because the problem never says anything about Jill's age two years ago.]

Exercise

A

In the following problem, there are several unknown lengths of time. It would therefore be incorrect to define a variable *t* to mean "time" without any further explanation. Look at the problem, decide how many different unknown times there are, and define each of those unknown times as a variable (DO NOT SOLVE THIS PROBLEM! JUST DEFINE THE VARIABLES):

Otto Biography can paint a particular house in 3 hours less than Adam Bomb can paint it. Working together, they can paint the house in $5\frac{1}{3}$ hours less than it takes Otto. How long does it take Adam to paint the house?

▶ **RULE 4: Whenever possible, define your variables using the exact same words and phrases as are used in the statement of the problem.**

EXAMPLE

 The first of two numbers is 18 larger than the second. Twice the first number is 15 more than three times the second. Find the two numbers.

SOLUTION:

Following Rule 2, we know that it would be wrong to say "x = a number," because there are two numbers in this problem. Specifically, these numbers are described as "the first number" and "the second number". Therefore, we describe the two numbers as follows:

x = the first number
y = the second number

(Again, it's true that we could describe both numbers while using only one variable, but we'll talk about that in the next chapter.)

Exercise

B

CAREFULLY define the variables in the following problem:

The sum of three consecutive even integers is 114. What are the integers?

Often a problem makes no direct reference to the unknown quantities. Suppose we have this problem:

EXAMPLE

A Cadillac costs $9,400 more than a Chevrolet. Three Chevrolets cost the same as two Cadillacs. How much does each car cost?

SOLUTION:

The two unknown quantities here are the price of a Cadillac, and the price of a Chevrolet. (Remember that the unknowns are not Cadillac and Chevrolet, because Cadillacs and Chevrolets are cars, not numbers.) But the statement doesn't use the word "price." If we are uncertain about what is being said about each quantity, we can rewrite the problem using the phrases "price of a Chevrolet" and "price of a Cadillac":

The price of a Cadillac is $9,400 more than the price of a Chevrolet. Three times the price of a Chevrolet is the same as two times the price of a Cadillac. What is the price of each car?

Now it becomes clear that our variables can be defined as:

x = price of a Cadillac
y = price of a Chevrolet

This idea will be even more helpful to us later, when we talk about setting up equations **(WHICH WE DO NOT DO UNTIL AFTER WE HAVE DEFINED OUR VARIABLES!** Remember?).

Exercise

Rewrite the following problem so that the unknown quantities are specifically referred to in the problem statement. Then define the variables (again, do not try to solve the problem!):

Jack Spratt is 85 pounds heavier than his wife. When they stand on a scale together, the scale reads 395 pounds. How much does Jack weigh alone?

In the problems we have examined so far, the unknown quantities were comparatively easy to spot. However, story problems frequently have "hidden" unknown quantities. Very often, identifying those hidden quantities is the key to solving the problem. To solve problems with hidden unknown quantities (in fact to solve any word problem), we need:

RULE 5: Every relevant unknown quantity must be explicitly described and defined.

Applying Rule 5

We will illustrate the application of Rule 5 by looking at a variety of problems. While the emphasis is on Rule 5, remember that the other four rules also play a part in defining the variables.

Coin Problems

Coin problems are popular with teachers and math textbook writers (but not necessarily with students!). They usually go something like this:

> *Jenny's coin purse contains 28 coins, all nickels and quarters. The total value of the coins is $2.40. How many of each kind of coin does she have?*

We will avoid the most common difficulties in problems of this kind if we carefully observe Rules 2, 3, and 5 above. First of all, we now know that it would be a serious offense to write:

$$N = \text{nickels}$$
$$Q = \text{quarters}$$

because nickels and quarters are not numbers! To do it correctly, we must write:

$$N = \textit{number of nickels}$$
$$Q = \textit{number of quarters}$$

Once we have defined the variables N and Q appropriately, we take another, closer look at the problem. Have we defined all the variable or unknown quantities in the problem? The answer is no; there is also information about the *value* of the coins. This is a good example of why it is so important to define each variable clearly and explicitly, so we don't mislead ourselves into believing that a variable stands for anything it doesn't stand for. The *number* of nickels is obviously not the same thing as the *value* of the nickels. For example, if the number of nickels is 2, then the value of the nickels would be 10 cents. Therefore we need to define variables, or algebraic expressions, to represent the value of the nickels and the value of the quarters.

How do we know that we need variables or expressions to represent the values of the coins? After all, a word problem might possibly have dozens of numeric quantities associated with it; how do we know which ones are relevant to the solution of the problem? To answer that question, ask yourself how we would proceed if we paid attention only to the number of coins. The only thing we know about the number is that there is a total of 28 coins. Clearly, that's not enough information to solve the problem. There could be 1 quarter and 27 nickels, or 14 quarters and 14 nickels, or any other combination adding up to 28. Our only hope of solving the problem is to use the information about the value of the coins, which is given as $2.40.

For the time being, we can simply use two more letters to stand for the values of the nickels and quarters:

> N = number of nickels
> Q = number of quarters
> V = total value of all the nickels
> W = total value of all the quarters

It's a good idea to write the words "total" and "all" in the definitions of V and W. That way you won't be tempted to think the V stands for the value of ONE nickel. (Of course, if V stood for the value of one nickel, then we would have $V = .05$, in which case V would not be an unknown quantity. We wouldn't need a variable for it at all.)

Just as in the previous examples, we could have defined all four quantities using only two variables (or even one), and we will devote an entire chapter to that subject later on.

Costs of Different Items

Problems such as the following are similar to the coin problem examined above.

Tickets for a flight from Dallas to San Francisco are $363 for adults and $242 for children. A plane took off with a full load of 168 passengers, and the total ticket sales were $57,717. How many adults and how many children were aboard?

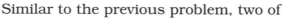

Similar to the previous problem, two of the unknown quantities are the *number* of adults and the *number* of children. But two additional quantities must be defined.

Exercise

Define the other two quantities (in addition to the number of adults and the number of children) which are necessary to solve the problem above.

Mixture Problems

Another common story problem is the mixture problem. A typical mixture problem is:

> *How many pounds of $6.00-per-pound nuts and how many pounds of $4.50-per-pound nuts need to be combined to make 18 pounds of a nut mixture which is worth $5.75 per pound?*

As before, we can see easily that we need to define variables or expressions for the number of pounds of $6.00-per-pound nuts and the amount of $4.50-per-pound nuts. But, just as in the previous problems, we have other quantities to define as well.

Exercise

Define the other two quantities (in addition to the number of pounds of each of the two kinds of nuts) which are necessary to solve the "nut" problem above.

 Solution and Alloy Problems

Another type of problem which has a "hidden" quantity to define is the solution/alloy problem. Here is an example:

> *A chemical manufacturer wants to mix some 10% pesticide solution with some 2% pesticide solution, so that the resulting mixture is 500 gallons of a 4.5% pesticide solution. How much of the 2% pesticide solution and how much of the 10% pesticide solution should be used?*

In this case, the obvious unknown quantities are the amounts of 2% pesticide solution and 10% pesticide solution to be used. But a little bit of thinking will tell us that simply defining the quantities of solution to be used will not be enough to solve the problem. Obviously, we could use any amounts of 2% solution and 10% solution, as long as they added up to 500 gallons—just as we could have added any numbers of nickels and quarters adding up to 28 in the earlier coin problem. The important requirement here is that we end up with a solution which is 4.5% pesticide.

We ask ourselves: How do we calculate the percentage of pesticide in a solution? The answer is: we divide the **amount of pure pesticide** by the total amount of the solution. Therefore, in order to calculate the percentage of pesticide in our final mixture, we will need to know both the amount of pure pesticide in the 2% solution, and the amount of pure pesticide in the 10% solution.

Let us note here that we don't need a variable or expression to represent the amount of pure pesticide in the final mixture. That's because the amount of pure pesticide in the final mixture is NOT an unknown quantity! We know we are going to end up with 500 gallons of the solution, and we also know that the final mixture will be 4.5% pesticide. Therefore we can calculate exactly how much pure pesticide there will be in the final mixture: .045(500) = 22.5 gallons.

To summarize, we are going to need the following variables (or expressions):

A = the amount of 2% pesticide solution to be used
B = the amount of 10% pesticide solution to be used
C = the amount of pure pesticide in the 2% solution used
D = the amount of pure pesticide in the 10% solution used

Once again, it is possible to define all these quantities using just two variables or even one, but we will discuss that in a later section.

Exercise

Read the following problem and define the quantities which need to be represented by variables or expressions. Note the similarity between this problem and the one above, but also note the difference!

A chemical manufacturer wants to mix some 10% pesticide solution with 500 gallons of a 2% pesticide solution, so that the resulting mixture is a 4.5% pesticide solution. How much of the 10% pesticide solution should be used?

 Multi-digit Integer Problems

One more device for torturing algebra students is a problem like the following:

The sum of the digits of a two-digit number is 11. If the digits are reversed, the new number will be 45 less than the original. What is the number?

The one obvious unknown quantity in this problem is the two-digit number itself. In fact, of course, if we knew the value of that two-digit number we would know everything there is to know about the quantities in the problem, and we would have the problem solved. But if we look carefully at the given information, we can see that the problem refers to three other unknown quantities besides the original two-digit number. For one thing, the problem talks about the sum of the two digits, and that can be represented only if we have defined each of the two digits separately. Furthermore, the problem talks about the value of the number we get when we reverse the digits. Therefore, we need to define that number (with the reversed digits) as an unknown quantity also. The lineup of unknown quantities is then:

> F = the first digit
> S = the second digit
> N = the original two-digit number
> R = the two-digit number we get by reversing the digits

 ### Problems Which Use Formulas

If the problem involves a formula (such as $A = lw$ for the area of a rectangle, or $rt = d$ for rate, time, and distance problems), then you will need to have either a number or a variable specifically assigned for each variable in the formula.

> *The simple interest on an account overr a period of 2 years was $89.70. The account paid an annuall interest at the rate of 5.75%. How much was originally in the account?*

The formula for simple interest is $I = Prt$, where I stands for the (amount of) interest, P is the principal (the amount originally in the account), r is the annual interest rate (and we have to remember to convert the percentage to a decimal!), and t is the length of time (measured in years) for which interest is being paid.

In this case, we are given values for I, r, and t. P is the unknown. The clearest way to organize the problem is:

> $I = 89.70$
> P = unknown
> $r = .0575$
> $t = 2$

It is true that we are defining only one unknown here; the other three values are given to us. But when we are going to use a formula, it is best to have the values laid out for every variable in the formula. Also, if we are going to use the formula only once, and unless there is additional information, we must have a numeric value for every variable in the formula except one. Despite the fact that you may think you have learned to solve equations which have more than one unknown, it isn't really true. Every algebraic method for solving equations with more than one unknown involves reducing the situation to an equation with only one unknown first.

In this case, we have values for every variable in the formula, so we are on the road to success!

Define the values and variables necessary to solve the following problem, using the formula

$$V = lwh$$

for the volume of a rectangular box.

A rectangular box with a square base is 14 inches high, and its volume is 350 cubic inches. What are the dimensions of the base?

More Than One Occurrence of the Same Formula

One of the most confusing situations students encounter occurs when a formula must be used more than once in the same problem. Look at the following problem:

> *The area of a rectangle is 108 square feet. If the length is increased by 1 and the width is decreased by 1, the area will be 104 square feet. What are the dimensions of the rectangle?*

We will use the formula $A = lw$ for the area of a rectangle, but we must recognize that we are going to use the formula twice, because there are two different rectangles in this problem! Therefore we set up the values and variables this way:

First rectangle:
$$A = 108$$
$$l = x$$
$$w = y$$

Second rectangle:
$$A = 104$$
$$l = z$$
$$w = v$$

(Once again, we admit that we can easily use "$x + 1$" and "$y - 1$" instead of z and v respectively for the second rectangle, but right now we are restricting the discussion to identifying the separate values and letters we are to use.)

A useful note: When using a formula more than once, it is probably best NOT to use the letters in the formula itself as variables. If we had used the letters l and w for the length and width of the first rectangle, we might be tempted to use them as the length and width of the second rectangle as well. That would cause trouble. We would also place ourselves eventually in the uncomfortable position of defining the length of our second rectangle as "$l = l + 1$," an equation which makes no sense.

Rate, Time, and Distance Problems

The need for using the same formula more than once is extremely common in problems like this one:

Bob Gorkle left for a bicycle trip at 8:00 AM, cycling at 12 mph. Penny Jarkle followed Bob 30 minutes later, leaving from the same point, and caught up with him at 10:30 AM. How fast was Penny going?

The standard formula for rate, time, and distance problems is $rt = d$, where r stands for the rate (speed), t stands for time, and d stands for distance. However, it is important to understand that the formula $rt = d$ applies to only one trip at a time, in which the speed is constant throughout. This problem deals with *two* trips: Bob's and Penny's. Therefore, we have two r's, two t's, and two d's. We set up the values and variables this way:

Bob's trip:

$r = 12$ (given)
$t = 2.5$ (two and a half hours from 8:00 to 10:30)
$d = x$ (unknown)

Penny's trip:

$r = y$ (unknown)
$t = 2$ (two hours from 8:30 to 10:30)
$d = x$ (we can use the same variable for the distance as we did in Bob's trip! Why??)

We have two unknown variables here, x and y, but that's OK because we will have two equations using the formula $rt = d$. [By the way, the reason we were allowed to use x to represent both the distance in Bob's trip and the distance in Penny's trip is that they traveled the same distance! The only way Penny could have caught up with Bob is if she had covered the same distance he had covered. We aren't always this lucky, of course, but if we know that two unknown quantities are equal, then we will always save ourselves trouble in the long run by assigning the same letter to both quantities.]

 Variation Problems

Variation problems are very much like formula problems which involve more than one occurrence of a formula. There are three kinds of variation:

1. If quantity Q_1 varies *directly* with (or as) quantity Q_2, then there is some number k for which the formula

$$Q_1 = kQ_2$$

always holds.

2. If quantity Q_1 varies *inversely* with (or as) quantity Q_2, then there is some number k for which the formula

$$Q_1 = \frac{k}{Q_2}$$

always holds.

3. If quantity Q_1 varies *jointly* with (or as) quantity Q_2 and Q_3, then there is some k number for which the formula

$$Q_1 = kQ_2Q_3$$

always holds.

Here is an example:

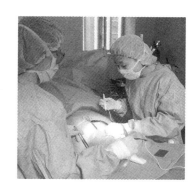

The amount of medication to be administered to a patient varies directly with the patient's weight. If the dosage of a 100-lb. person is 3 mg., then how much should be given to a 175-lb. person?

The statement that "the amount of medication to be administered to a patient varies directly with the patient's weight" tells us what the quantities Q_1 and Q_2 are. Q_1 stands for the amount of medication (the dosage), and Q_2 stands for the patient's weight. The first statement in the problem, therefore, says that $Q_1 = 3$ when $Q_2 = 100$. Then we are asked for the value of Q_1 when $Q_2 = 175$. We set up our variables the same way we did when we had two occurrences of the same formula:

First occurrence:

$Q_1 = 3$
$Q_2 = 100$
$k =$ unknown (we can use the k letter in both occurrences because it will be the same value both times)

Second occurrence:

$Q_1 = x$ (unknown)
$Q_2 = 175$
$k = k$ (same value as in the first occurrence above)

Sometimes a variation problem is more complex, with one quantity varying directly or jointly with some quantities and inversely with others.

The number of phone calls between two cities each business day varies jointly with the populations of the two cities, and inversely with the square of the distance between the cities. Dweebville has a population of 10,000. Dork Springs, 25 miles away, has a population of 20,000. There are approximately 8,000 calls each business day between the two cities. About how many calls per day will there be between Kansas City (population 435,000) and St. Louis (population 397,000), 260 miles apart?

The first sentence this time says that Q_1 is the number of phone calls each day between the two cities, and that Q_2, Q_3 and Q_4 are the population of the first city, the population of the second city, and the distance between the cities respectively. Furthermore, we are told that Q_1 varies jointly with Q_2 and Q_3, and inversely with $(Q_4)^2$. That means our formula will be:

$$Q_1 = \frac{Q_2 Q_3}{(Q_4)^2} k$$

In the first occurrence of the variation formula, we have:

Q_1 = 8,000
Q_2 = 10,000
Q_3 = 20,000
Q_4 = 25
k = unknown (once again we can use the same letter, k, for both occurrences)

The second occurrence of the formula will use these values:

Q_1 = x (unknown)
Q_2 = 435,000
Q_3 = 397,000
Q_4 = 260
k = k (value will come from the first occurrence)

 Percent Problems

Most all percent problems involve three primary quantities:

1. The percent itself, which usually comes immediately before the word "percent" in the problem statement.

2. The quantity on which the percent is based. This quantity often follows the word "of" in the statement of the problem, and is referred to as the "base."

3. The quantity which is some percent or fraction of the base. We will sometimes refer to this as the "percent quantity"; **it is important to distinguish the percent quantity from the percent itself!**

Here is an example:

Baseball player Steve Orino got hits in 23 out of 89 official at bats. What percent of his at bats were hits?

24

The three quantities are:

x = percent (unknown)
89 = at bats (base)
23 = hits (percent quantity)

 Percent Increases and Decreases

When a quantity increases or decreases by a percent, the percent quantity is neither the original number nor the new number. It is *the difference between the old and new numbers*. And, the "base" is **always the old number**.

Here is an example:

The price of a new car has been reduced by 7%. The new price is $20,088. What was the original price?

Quantities:

7 = percent
x = old quantity (old price)
y = percent quantity (7% of old price)

So what do we do with the $20,088? Doesn't it have anything to do with the problem? The answer is yes, it's very important. But it isn't any of the three primary quantities we deal with in percent problems. We will use the $20,088 in the next chapter to reduce the number of variables in this problem from two to one.

 Exponential Growth and Decay
(for students with a knowledge of logarithms)

Perhaps the most common type of word problem which involves using the same formula more than once is the exponential growth or decay problem. We almost always need to use the standard formula:

$$Q = Q_0 e^{kt} \text{ (for exponential growth)}$$
$$\text{or}$$
$$Q = Q_0 e^{-kt} \text{ (for exponential decay)}$$

twice in order to solve the problem. [Note: Some books use only the first formula above, whether the problem involves growth or decay. In that case the constant turns out to be negative for decay problems. So the exponent ends up being negative for decay problems regardless of which book you read.]

Read the following problem:

In 1910 the population of Kentucky was 2.28 million. In 1940 the population was 2.85 million. If the population continued to grow at the same constant rate that it averaged from 1910 to 1940, what should the population have been in 1990?

Most students are aware from the beginning that they must use the exponential growth formula given above to solve this problem. The reason they have trouble is that they don't realize that they must use the formula *twice*. How do we know we need to use it twice? Because the problem talks about two different periods of growth: the period from 1910 to 1940, and the period from 1940 (or from 1910) to 1990. The formula is appropriate only for one period at a time.

If we try to use the formula only once, we will run into difficulty. For one thing, there will be two unknowns: k and Q. And we know that we cannot solve one equation for two unknowns. Furthermore, we will get ourselves terribly confused when we try to decide what the original quantity Q_0 is. Is it the population in 1910, or the population in 1940? And regardless of which one it is, what must we do with the other number?

The correct procedure is to use the formula once to describe the growth from 1910 to 1940, and use it again to describe the growth from 1940 to 1990. Setting up the values of the variables:

1910 to 1940:

Q = 2.85 million
Q_0 = 2.28 million
k = unknown
t = 30 (for the 30 years between 1910 and 1940)

Please note that e is <u>not</u> a variable or an unknown. It is a constant number, the same in every problem, equal to about 2.718.

1940 to 1990:

$Q = x$ (unknown)
Q_0 = 2.85 million
k = unknown
t = 50 (for the 50 years between 1940 and 1990)

We are allowed to use the same letter k in both occurrences of the formula, because k will have the same value for both periods of growth. In fact, that is exactly what the problem means when it says, "If the population continued to grow at the same constant rate that it averaged from 1910 to 1940...". It is k which describes the rate of growth. One further comment is necessary to set up for the second growth period: We might just as well have decided to use 1910 to 1990 as our second growth period (instead of 1940 to 1990). If we had, then Q_0 would have been 2.28 million, and t would have been 80 (the time period between 1910 and 1990). Honestly and truly, we would wind up with the same answer either way. It would not be correct, however, to change anything in the first growth period. That one has to be 1910 to 1940, because that's the only period for which we know the population at both the beginning and the end.

Looking at the two setups of variables, we see that the first occurrence of the formula will have only one unknown, namely k. Therefore we will be able to solve for k; and by the time we use the formula the second time, k will no longer be unknown. The second use of the formula, then, will enable us to solve for the real unknown, x.

 Notes about Half-lives

Many students are confused by problems like this:

> The half-life of a particular radioactive material is 29 days. How long will it take 100 grams to decay down to 15 grams?

There are two points to be made:

1. The half-life is the <u>length of time</u> it takes for the material to decay down to half its original size. Therefore, when we set up the variables for the formula $Q = Q_0 e^{-kt}$, the half-life will be used as a value for t.

2. For any quantity which decreases according to the exponential formula, the time it takes to decrease to half its original size will be the same regardless of what the original quantity is. Therefore, the statement "The half-life of a particular radioactive material is 29 days" is equivalent to saying that "If we start with an 88-gram sample of the material, the sample will have decayed down to 44 grams after 29 days." It is also equivalent to saying, "If we start with a 1-gram sample of the material, the sample will have decayed down to $\frac{1}{2}$ gram after 29 days." In other words, when setting up the first occurrence of the formula, you can use any number you want for Q_0, as long as you use exactly half that number for Q. You will find, however, that the equation is easiest to solve if you use $Q_0 = 1$ and $Q = \frac{1}{2}$.

   To set up this problem, the first decay period is 29 days long, and the values of the variables in the formula would be:

   $Q = \frac{1}{2}$
   $Q_0 = 1$
   $k = k$ (unknown)
   $t = 29$

For the second occurrence, the values would be:

$$Q = 15$$
$$Q_0 = 100$$
$$k = k \text{ (unknown, but we will know it from the first}$$
$$\text{occurrence by the time we need it)}$$
$$t = x \text{ (unknown)}$$

Exercise

Set up the values of the variables in the exponential growth formula for the following problem:

The population of Hogwash County doubles every 55 years. If the population was 87,000 in 1960, what was the population in 1996?

▶ **Intermediate Variables**

Sometimes it is difficult or impossible to find the value of the unknown quantity directly, but if you knew the value of some other quantity, you would be able to solve the problem. In some problems, that other quantity isn't even mentioned directly, and you have to figure it out for yourself. We call such a quantity an intermediate variable.

Here is an example:

The area of a circle is 2,463 square inches. What is the circumference?

The unknown quantity here, of course, is the circumference. Tragically, however, we have no commonly known formula for figuring out the circumference when we know the area. What we do have is a formula for the circumference if we know the radius—namely, $C = 2\pi r$. Therefore, we define a variable for the radius of the circle, even though the problem never mentions the radius. In fact, since we have formulas for both the area and the circumference of a circle, we will establish our quantities with reference to those formulas:

Formula for area: $A = \pi r^2$
    $A = 2463$
        $r = r$ (it's OK to use the letter r in this case because r will be the same radius of the same circle in both formulas)

Formula for circumference: $C = 2\pi r$
    $C = C$ (unknown)
        $r = r$

In the formula for the circumference, both variables are unknown, but that's OK because once again we will have two equations with two unknowns. The procedure will be to solve the area formula for r and then use that value in the circumference formula. Please note that π not a variable, and it is not unknown! It is equal to about 3.14159, and can be retrieved from most calculators. It is much like the number e in that respect.

Here is a further example:

An Internet service provider finds that 5000 people will subscribe to its service if the charge is $35 per month. They estimate that for each $1 reduction in the monthly fee, an additional 600 more people will subscribe. What price should they charge in order to get $257,600 in monthly revenue?

This type of problem produces much weeping, wailing, and gnashing of teeth among students. The reason for the difficulty is that they easily see that one of the unknown quantities is the monthly fee (after all, that's the number the problem asks you to calculate). With slightly more effort, they see that the number of subscribers is another unknown quantity. Further strenuous thought shows that the total monthly revenue ($257,600) is going to be the product of the number of subscribers times the monthly fee. However, that gives us two unknowns and only one equation.

The way out of this difficulty is to realize that there is an intermediate variable, which, if we knew its value, would give us both the number of subscribers and the monthly fee. That variable is <u>the number of $1 decreases from the original $35 fee</u>.

Let's be specific. We let D = the number of $1 decreases from the original $35 fee. Suppose then that $D = 6$. Then the monthly fee would be $35 – $6 = $29. Since we add 600 new people for each $1 decrease in the fee, we must be adding $6 \times 600 = 3,600$ new subscribers in addition to the 5,000 we had when the fee was $35. The new number of subscribers is 5,000 + 3,600 = 8,600.

Conversely, if we know the number of subscribers, we can figure out D. For example, if there were 6,200 subscribers, that would mean an increase of 1200 over the original 5,000. That, in turn, would mean we must have reduced the fee by $2 (1,200 divided by 600). Therefore D would be 2. And, of course, once we know the value of D, it's a simple matter to calculate the new monthly fee. If D is 2, then the new monthly fee is $35 – $2 = $33.

Therefore our three unknown quantities in this problem are:
S = number of subscribers
F = monthly fee
D = number of $1 reductions from the original $35 fee

Our informal discussion above shows that if we know the value of D, we will be able to calculate S and F, which means we will be able to reduce the three unknowns to only one when we talk about problems like this in the next section.

"Betty Can Do a Job in 10 Hours..." Problems

Let's look again at a problem we saw earlier in this chapter:

> *Otto Biography can paint a particular house in 3 hours less than Adam Bomb can paint it. Working together, they can paint the house in $5\frac{1}{3}$ hours less than it takes Otto. How long does it take Adam to paint the house?*

Problems of this type have a fiendishly well-hidden quantity associated with them. To see why we need an additional quantity, we need to look ahead to consider how we are going to solve this problem. When we talk about Adam and Otto working together, it is fairly clear that we are adding something, but exactly *what* are we adding? We are certainly *not* adding Otto's time plus Adam's time. If Adam has Otto's help, that certainly isn't going to *increase* the amount of time it takes! (Remember common sense!)

Subtracting one time from the other isn't the right idea either. To see why that won't work, imagine that Adam and Otto both took the same amount of time. In that case, if we subtracted one person's time from the other person's, we would get zero—and they can't be expected to do the job in zero hours, even working together.

OK, OK—here's the missing quantity: *The proportion (or fraction) of the entire job which each person, or the two of them working together, can do in one hour.* The reason we need this quantity is that it is the <u>work</u> which is being added together when Adam and Otto both work together. For example, if Adam did $\frac{1}{10}$ of the job in an hour and Otto did $\frac{1}{7}$ of the job in one hour, then together they would do $\frac{1}{10} + \frac{1}{7} = \frac{17}{70}$ of the job.

Therefore, in this problem we have six quantities (although very soon we will be able to express all six of them using only one variable):

> A = time taken by Adam working alone
> B = time taken by Otto working alone
> T = time taken by Adam and Otto working together
> W = fraction of the entire job done by Adam in 1 hour
> X = fraction of the entire job done by Otto in 1 hour
> Z = fraction of the entire job done by Adam and Otto
>   together in 1 hour

Final Thoughts

This chapter is the most important section in the book! If the quantities are not defined correctly, nothing you can do during the rest of the process is going to make up for that. And if the quantities <u>are</u> defined correctly, the rest of the process is much easier.

It is important that the definitions of the quantities be written down clearly and fully, where you can refer to them throughout the rest of the process.

In reality, you will sometimes find yourself getting far along in the process of solving a problem, and then realize that you needed to define a quantity which you didn't think of at the beginning. That's all right; it's not always possible to anticipate every quantity you need at this stage of the game. On the other hand, you will sometimes find that you have defined quantities which you don't need when you get to the stage of setting up equations and solving them. That's all right too. The more experience you gain, the more often you will be able to identify on the first try exactly those quantities you will need in order to solve the problem. The important thing is to realize and understand that the defining of your quantities is a **vital and <u>separate</u>** step in solving word problems. You can't just slide over the step, figuring that the quantities to use will be obvious once you get to the equation. That's just not true!

Exercise

In all cases, assign a letter (variable) to each unknown relevant quantity in the problem. Do not try to solve the problems. Also, do not try to reduce the number of variables or to define one unknown quantity in terms of another. We will work on that in the next chapter.

1. The price of a computer has been reduced by 16%. The original price was $2,700. What is the new price?

2. If 5 cooks can prepare a banquet for 100 people in $3\frac{1}{2}$ hours, then how long does it take 7 cooks to prepare a banquet for 175 people? (Assume the time taken varies directly with the number of people to be fed, and inversely with the number of cooks.)

3. Rosita deposited $1,400 in the bank on January 1, 1990. She closed the account on January 2, 1992, and withdrew the entire account balance of $1,533. What was the interest rate?

4. Reversing the digits of a three-digit number will cause the number to increase by 297. The third digit of the original number is equal to the sum of the first two digits, and is also 2 less than twice the second digit. What is the original number?

5. During a one-hour period, a toll bridge collected $164.50 in tolls from 97 vehicles. The bridge toll is $1.00 for cars and $2.50 for trucks. How many cars and how many trucks crossed the bridge?

6. Michael is 3 years older than his brother Nick. In two years, he will be twice as old as Nick. How old is Nick?

7. Ludwig wants 65 pounds of mixed nuts, of which 35% will be peanuts. He has available to him a mixture which is 52% peanuts and another mixture which is 30% peanuts. How much of each mixture should he use?

8. Marian began driving west along Interstate 70 from St. Louis at 10:00 AM. Her husband George began driving east from Kansas City, along the same highway, at 10:45 AM. The distance from St. Louis to Kansas City is 256 miles. George averaged 68 mph, and the two of them met at 12:20 PM. How fast was Marian driving?

9. When the height of a triangle was increased by 1 foot and the base was decreased by 1 foot, the area increased from 96 square feet to 99 square feet. What were the original dimensions of the triangle?

10. Stan can drive his math teacher out of his mind in 35 minutes. Leonard can do it in 45 minutes. If Stan and Leonard combine their efforts, how long will it take before their distinguished teacher runs from the classroom?

11. Nerdley is trying to sell copies of a math textbook to a college bookstore. He will sell them for $58.00 each. But if the store will buy more than 50 copies, he will reduce the price per book by 50¢ for each 10 additional copies (over 50) that the bookstore buys—until the price gets down to $35.00. How many copies does the bookstore have to buy in order to pay a total of $6,500?

REDUCING THE NUMBER OF VARIABLES

As we have seen, many word problems involve more than one unknown quantity. Often, information is given in the problem which relates one of the unknown quantities to another. We can usually use this information to reduce the number of variables we are dealing with. Although it is OK to define each separate quantity with a separate variable, it is usually easiest to minimize the number of variables we deal with.

 Comparing Two Quantities

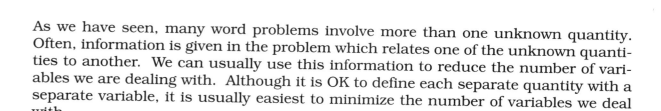

Suppose you refer to a particular unknown quantity as *x*.

How would you refer to a second quantity which is 5 more than the first quantity?

SOLUTION: *x* + 5.

Exercise

Assume that you have already defined the variable *n* to stand for a particular unknown quantity mentioned in a word problem. Give the algebraic expressions which would define the following quantities:

    a. 2 less than the unknown quantity.
    b. 5 times the unknown quantity.
    c. The difference between the unknown quantity and 18.
    d. The difference between 18 and the unknown quantity.
    e. The quotient of 64 and the unknown quantity.
    f. 64 divided by the unknown quantity.
    g. 64 divided into the unknown quantity.

Please notice that when the given phrase calls for subtraction or division, **it makes a difference which quantity is mentioned first**. "The difference between *a* and *b*" is *a* − *b*. But "the difference between *b* and *a*" is *b* − *a*. Similarly, "the quotient of *a* and *b*" and "*a* divided by *b*" are both described by the fraction $\frac{a}{b}$. But "*a* divided into *b*" is $\frac{b}{a}$.

We need not worry about order when we talk about addition or multiplication, because those operations are *commutative*: $a \cdot b$ is the same as $b \cdot a$, and $a + b$ is the same as $b + a$.

More Complicated Combinations

If we have already defined an unknown number by the variable x, then how would we describe the following quantities?

1. Ten less than the square of the unknown number.

2. Ten less than the number squared.

3. Ten less than the number, squared.

The answers to #1 and #2 are the same: $x^2 - 10$. In the first case, we would reason as follows: I am being asked for 10 less than <u>something</u>. What is the "something"? The "something" is the square of the unknown number. In other words, the "something" is x^2. Therefore, I am being asked for 10 less than x^2, which is $x^2 - 10$.

In #2, I would have to remember my *order of operations* —that is, the rule which tells me that exponents come before subtraction. The description of the quantity we are trying to describe involves both subtraction and exponentiation. But since exponents come before subtraction, I would first attach the exponent to the unknown number, that is, make the x into an x^2, before applying the subtraction. So I would end up, again, with $x^2 - 10$.

The only difference between #2 and #3 is one little comma, after the word "number." But that one little comma makes all the difference. The comma means take ten less than the number first, *before* you square anything. Therefore the answer would be $(x-10)^2$, or $x^2 - 20x + 100$. [No readers of this book would *ever* think that $(x - 10)^2$ is $x^2 - 100$, would they?]

Exercise

Assume that you have already defined the variable x to stand for "an unknown number." Build algebraic expressions for the following quantities:

a. The difference between 25 and the quotient of an unknown number and 4.

b. The quotient of 25 and the difference between an unknown number and 4.

c. The sum of 17 and the square of an unknown number.

d. The sum of 17 and an unknown number, divided by the difference between 36 and the unknown number.

EXAMPLE

○ Consider the following problem:

Cheryl bicycled at 12 mph for some length of time, and then slowed down to 9 mph for the last 2 hours of her trip. She found that she had covered a total of 39 miles. If T represents the length of time she bicycled at 12 mph, how do we describe the total duration (time) of the trip?

SOLUTION: $T + 2$.

Exercise

If B stands for your checkbook balance, and you write 3 checks for $23.79 each, what is the new balance?

EXAMPLE

○ *Mary is 7 years older than Jill. If J stands for Jill's age, what expression should we use for Mary's age?*

SOLUTION:

This is another problem which can be made clearer by rewriting the problem so that it refers directly to the unknown quantities (see the previous chapter for more examples of this idea):

 Mary's age is 7 years more than Jill's age.

Now it becomes clear that if J is Jill's age, then Mary's age is $J + 7$.

The previous example illustrates a point which is easy to miss. The given information in the problem said "Mary is 7 years older than Jill." We decided, without explanation, to let J stand for Jill's age and then define Mary's age in terms of J. Could we have done it the other way around? That is, could we have said:

 M = Mary's age

and then figured out what Jill's age is in terms of M (in other words, as an algebraic expression involving M)?

The answer is yes, we could have, **but** it would have been a bit more difficult. We would have reasoned as follows:

> Since Mary is 7 years older than Jill, that means Jill is 7 years <u>younger</u> than Mary. Therefore Jill's age is 7 years less than Mary's age. So Jill's age must be $M - 7$.

This experience leads to **a strong suggestion** (but not an ironclad rule):

> If the information in a problem includes a comparison between two quantities, then it is usually easiest to let your variable (letter) stand for the *second* quantity, and then define the first quantity in terms of that variable.

Exercise

Define the unknown quantities in the following statement, using only one variable:

When George and Peter ride their bicycles, George travels 4 miles per hour faster than Peter. (Don't forget that if you say "P = Peter," you're <u>already wrong!!</u>)

Several special situations comparing two quantities are worth discussing separately.

 When One Quantity Is a Fraction of Another

When we are talking about a fraction of a quantity, the word "of" translates into *times* (multiplication).

> *Holly spent one-fourth of her paycheck on rent. Define the unknown quantities, using only one variable.*

To solve the problem, let P = amount of Holly's paycheck.

Then, $\frac{1}{4}P$ = amount Holly spent on rent.

 Percents

A percent is just a fraction with a denominator of 100. We often express a percent as a decimal fraction; for example, 29% can be written either as $\frac{29}{100}$ or as 0.29.

> *Hugh's suit cost 87% as much as Elizabeth's dress. Define the two unknown quantities, using only one variable.*

To solve the problem, Let E = cost of Elizabeth's dress.

Then, $0.87E$ = cost of Hugh's suit.

(We could also use $\frac{87}{100}E$, or $\frac{87E}{100}$.)

Notice that again we have chosen a variable, E, which stands for the quantity mentioned *second* (the cost of Elizabeth's dress), rather than the first quantity mentioned (the cost of Hugh's suit).

 Percent Increases and Decreases

If a quantity is increased or decreased by a given percent, the new quantity is equal to the old quantity, plus or minus the given percent *of the old quantity*. We mentioned earlier in Chapter 2 that the percent quantity in problems of this kind is always the difference between the old and new numbers.

Define the quantities for the following problem:

The price of a new car has been reduced by 7%. The new price is $20,088. What was the original price?

In solving the problem, P = original price of the car (the base), 7 = percent, and $P - 20,088$ = amount of decrease (also the percent quantity).

 When the Sum of Two Unknown Quantities Is Given

Try this exercise:

Feeble and Dweeble's ages add up to 78. If Feeble's age is 30, what is Dweeble's age?

After some thought, you probably will decide correctly that Dweeble's age is 48. And how did you figure that out? Probably by subtracting 78 minus 30. In other words, Dweeble's age is the sum of the two ages (78), minus Feeble's age (30). Now try this one:

Feeble and Dweeble's ages add up to 78. If Feeble's age is F, what is Dweeble's age?

This is one of those "have the courage of your convictions" examples. In the previous exercise you subtracted Feeble's age from the total. Is there any reason to do something different this time? None whatsoever. The answer is $78 - F$.

This example leads us to a fact which comes up again and again in word problems. We can state this fact in terms of the previous example:

If two quantities add up to 78, and one of the quantities is x, then the other quantity is $78 - x$. (Note that it's $78 - x$, and not $x - 78$!!)

Of course, there is nothing special about the number 78. We could have said the same thing about any two numbers which add up to any given total.

Unit Cost vs. Total Cost

Many problems involve both the individual price of one particular item (often referred to as the "unit cost"), and also the total price of a number of identical items. You almost certainly know how to handle this situation, even if you think you don't.

Exercise

If pears cost 59 cents each, how much would you have to pay for 6 pears?

Answer the question, **and** explain how you got your answer.

If you did the exercise correctly, you multiplied 59 by 6 and got 354 cents, or $3.54. In other words, you multiplied the price of each pear by the number of pears.

Exercise

*Using the same procedure as in the previous exercise, define an unknown number of pears, **and** the total cost of those pears, if the pears cost 59 cents each.*

The above exercise is an example of one of the most important themes in this book:

Have the courage of your convictions! If you decided that P stands for the number of pears, then whenever you're talking about the number of pears, you're talking about P. And whenever you're talking about P, you're talking about the number of pears. Anything you would do with the number of pears (if you knew the exact number), can also be done with the letter P.

In Exercise E you multiplied the price of each pear by the number of pears, which was 6. So in Exercise F, you should have done the exact same thing: multiply the price of each pear by the number of pears, <u>which was P.</u>

Putting the discussion above into **a simple rule**:

You can express the total <u>cost</u> of a number of identical items by multiplying the single price of each (the "unit cost") times the number of items being purchased. This rule applies whether the unit cost and number of items are known numbers or are variables.

Exercise

Define the individual cost of a cassette tape, and the total cost of 11 tapes, using only one variable.

Now let's reverse the situation:

The cost of a dozen boxes of chalk is C. What is the cost of one box?

Once again, ask yourself what you would do if you were given a specific number (like $3.24) for the total cost of a dozen boxes, instead of the letter C. The answer is, you would *divide* the $3.24 (the total cost of a dozen) by 12, and get the answer ($0.27). So once again, **have the courage of your convictions!** If the total cost is C instead of $3.24, you divide C by 12. The answer is then $\frac{C}{12}$.

In summary: The total cost is the unit cost *times* the number of items, and the unit cost is the total cost *divided* by the number of items. And those rules apply *regardless* of whether any of the three quantities (unit cost, number of items, and total cost) are given as numbers, or represented as variables!

Sometimes the comparison between one value and another is given in words which are not strictly mathematical, and we have to translate the given language into "more than," "less than," etc.

Number vs. Value

In Chapter 2, pages 6-17, we discussed the following problem:

Jenny's coin purse contains 28 coins, all nickels and quarters. The total value of the coins is $2.40. How many of each kind of coin does she have?

We decided that there were four unknown quantities, namely:

N = number of nickels V = total value of all the nickels
Q = number of quarters W = total value of all the quarters

We should now be able to reduce the four variables to only one. First of all, we know that the total number of coins is 28. That means that N and Q add up to 28. Accordingly, we can use $28 - N$ for the number of quarters, instead of Q. That brings us down to three variables:

N = number of nickels
$28 - N$ = number of quarters
V = total value of all the nickels
W = total value of all the quarters

Now we remember that we can get the total value of a number of identical items by multiplying the unit price (or value) times the number of items. The unit value of a nickel is 5 cents, and the unit value of a quarter is 25 cents. Therefore the total value in cents of all nickels is 5 times the number of nickels, or $5N$, and the total value of all the quarters is 25 times the number of quarters, or $25(28 - N)$. Suddenly we've done it! All four quantities can be expressed with just the letter N:

  N = number of nickels
  $28 - N$ = number of quarters
  $5N$ = total value of all the nickels
  $25(28 - N)$ = total value of all the quarters

Here is another example to illustrate Number vs. Value:

How many pounds of $6.00-per-pound nuts, and how many pounds of $4.50-per-pound nuts need to be combined to make 18 pounds of a nut mixture which is worth $5.75 per pound?

The problem says that we will end up with a total of 18 pounds of nuts; therefore the two unknown quantities add up to 18. So we can define our quantities this way:

  x = amount of $6.00-per-lb. nuts **(pounds)**
  $18 - x$ = amount of $4.50-per-lb. nuts (pounds)
  $6x$ = total dollar value of $6.00-per-lb. nuts
  $4.5(18 - x)$ = total dollar value of $4.50-per-lb. nuts

Exercise

In the following problem, suppose that C = the number of children's tickets sold. What expression would we use to describe the number of adult tickets sold?

Tickets for a flight from Dallas to San Francisco are $363 for adults and $242 for children. A plane took off with a full load of 168 passengers, and the total ticket sales were $57,717. How many adults and how many children were aboard?

 Solutions and Mixtures

Suppose we have P pounds of one alloy which is 15% copper, and Q pounds of a second alloy which is 28% copper.

 (a) How would we describe the amount of pure copper in each alloy?

 (b) How would we describe the amount of pure copper in the mixture we would get by putting the two alloys together?

Part (a) is nothing more than a percent problem like the ones we have already talked about. The amount of copper in the first alloy is $.15P$, and the amount of copper in the second alloy is $.28Q$.

Part (b) is simply the sum of the two expressions given in (a):
$.15P + 28Q$.

Read the following problem:

A chemical manufacturer wants to mix some 10% pesticide solution with 500 gallons of a 2% pesticide solution, so that the resulting mixture is a 4.5% pesticide solution. How much of the 10% pesticide solution should be used?

Now, if we let S = the amount of 10% pesticide solution to be used:

a. How will we designate the <u>amount of pesticide </u>in the 10% solution?

b. How will we designate the <u>total amount of the mixture</u>?

c. How will we designate the <u>total amount of *pesticide* in the mixture</u>?

Answer all three questions using only the letter S as a variable.

 Miscellaneous Problems

Below are examples of how to reduce the number of variables in some special problems types which do not fall easily into any of the preceeding categories.

 Tailwind/Headwind Problems

If a plane can go 235 mph in still air, and it is flying with a 40 mph tailwind, then the plane's speed with respect to the ground is 235 + 40 = 275 mph. If the plane is flying directly into a 40 mph wind, then its speed with respect to the ground is 235 – 40 = 195 mph.

The same principle applies to problems involving boats going upstream and downstream. If a boat which can be rowed at 6 mph is going upstream on a river flowing at 2 mph, then the speed with which the boat passes objects on the shore in 6 – 2 = 4 mph. If the same boat is going downstream, then its speed with respect to the shore is 6 + 2 = 8.

An airplane whose speed in still air is 250 mph flies against a headwind for 3 hours, and then turns around and returns with the wind. The airplane's total trip takes 5 hours and 15 minutes. If W represents the speed of the wind, how do we describe the speed of the plane (with respect to the ground) when it was flying with the wind, and how do we describe the speed when flying against the wind?

Consecutive Integer Problems

Suppose we talk about three *consecutive* integers, and we know that the first of the three integers is 15. What is the second integer, and what is the third? Obviously, the second integer is 16 and the third is 17.

The key is the word "consecutive." How did we get the numbers 16 and 17? Of course, we just started with the given, 15, added 1 to get 16, and added 1 more to get 17. Therefore, if we have three consecutive integers and the first integer is x, what are the second and third integers?

Answer: the second integer is $x + 1$ and the third integer is $x + 2$.

So, when we have problems dealing with (for example) three consecutive integers, we don't need to define the three integers as x, y, and z. We really need only one variable, x, to represent the first integer. Then the second integer is $x + 1$, and the third is $x + 2$.

Now, suppose we are talking about three consecutive *odd* integers, and the first one of them is 15. What are the other two integers? The second integer, naturally, is 17, and the third is 19.

How did we get the 17 and the 19 in this case? Well, we might have started with 15 and just gone through the integers until we came to another odd one. But if we are familiar with the number system, we know that every other number is odd, and that therefore the next odd number after 15 will be $15 + 2 = 17$. Using the same logic, the next (third) odd number will be $17 + 2 = 19$, or $15 + 4 = 19$.

Accordingly, when we deal with consecutive *odd* integer problems, we define the first integer as x, and then the others are $x + 2$, $x + 4$, $x + 6$, etc.

Exercise

Define the unknown quantities in the following problem, using only one variable **(Don't try to solve the problem!)**:

The sum of three consecutive even integers is 78. What are the three integers?

Multi-digit Integer Problems

Here is a problem we looked at in Chapter 2, pages 9-20:

The sum of the digits of a two-digit number is 11. If the digits are reversed, the new number will be 45 less than the original. What is the number?

We decided that there are four unknown quantities in this problem:

F = the first digit
S = the second digit
N = the original two-digit number
R = the number with the digits reversed

The problem would certainly be easier if we could reduce the number of variables from four to two, or even one. We can have our wish if we know the following rule:

If F stands for the first digit of a two-digit number and S stands for the second digit of the same number, then the value of the two-digit number itself is $10F + S$.

Similarly:

If F stands for the first digit of a <u>three</u>-digit number, S stands for the second digit, and T stands for the third digit, then the three-digit number itself is $100F + 10S + T$.

So now, for our problem, we can define our quantities as follows:

F = the first digit
S = the second digit
$10F + S$ = the original two-digit number
$10S + F$ = the number with the digits reversed

[Quick exercise: How did we get the $10S + F$ for the number with the digits reversed?]

Exercise

Look again at the problem we have been analyzing:

The sum of the digits of a two-digit number is 11. If the digits are reversed, the new number will be 45 less than the original. What is the number?

We have already reduced the number of variables to two, F and S. Now, using the fact that the sum of the digits is 11, express all four unknown quantities in terms of <u>one</u> variable.

 Ratios

The ratio of one quantity to a second quantity is a fraction, with the first quantity on top and the second quantity on the bottom.

The ratio of men to women in Professor Shockem's electrical engineering class is $1\frac{1}{2}$ times the ratio of men to women in Professor Tinear's music class. If there are 12

men and 12 women in the electrical engineering class, and a total of 35 students in the music class, how many men and how many women are in the music class?

The obvious quantities here are the numbers of men, women, and total students in each class. However, the problem also makes reference to the *ratio* of men to women in each class. We set up the quantities this way:

men in electrical engineering class = 12

women in electrical engineering class = 12

ratio of men to women in electrical engineering class = $\frac{12}{12}$ = 1

men in music class = M

women in music class = $35 - M$

ratio of men to women in music class = $\frac{M}{35-M}$

Revisiting Chapter 2: Defining the Quantities

We will now revisit several of the problems first discussed in Chapter 2 and describe how the number of variables can be reduced, in most cases, to only one.

EXAMPLES

Otto Biography can paint a particular house in 3 hours less than Adam Bomb can paint it. Working together, they can paint the house in $5\frac{1}{3}$ hours less than it takes Otto. How long does it take Adam to paint the house?

Originally, on page 14, all that the exercise asked of the reader was to define the different unknown "times" in the problem. There are, in fact, three different times, as we saw on page 30.

A = time taken by Adam working alone
B = time taken by Otto working alone
T = time taken by Adam and Otto working together

However, we now know enough to represent all three times using only one variable. If we find the process at all difficult, we can rewrite the problem using our unknown phrases explicitly, as we have done before:

The time it takes Otto Biography to paint a particular house is 3 hours less than the time it takes Adam Bomb to paint the same house. The time it takes Adam and Otto working together is $5\frac{1}{3}$ hours less than the time it takes Otto. How long does it take Adam to paint the house?

As above, we set up A = the time it takes Adam, as our main variable, since that is the quantity mentioned *second*. Because the time it takes Otto is 3 hours less than the time it takes Adam, we know that the time it takes Otto is $A - 3$:

A = time taken by Adam working alone
$A - 3$ = time taken by Otto working alone

Now, what do we use for the time it takes both of them working together to paint the house? That time is $5\frac{1}{3}$ hours less than the time it takes Otto; in other words, $5\frac{1}{3}$ hours less than $A - 3$. Therefore, the time it takes the two of them working together is $(A - 3) - 5\frac{1}{3}$, or $A - 8\frac{1}{3}$:

A = time taken by Adam working alone
$A - 3$ = time taken by Otto working alone
$A - 8\frac{1}{3}$ = time taken by Adam and Otto working together

We have now defined all three unknown times using only one variable. However, we also learned that we needed three other quantities: namely, the fraction of the entire house that each person, and the two of them working together, could paint in one hour. Can we express those three quantities in terms of just A also?

The answer is yes, we can. To see this, let's once again ask ourselves what we would do if Adam's time were given to us as a number instead of a variable. Suppose we knew that Adam took 20 hours to paint the house. Then what fraction of the house would he paint in 1 hour?

The answer is, of course, that Adam would paint $\frac{1}{20}$ of the house in 1 hour. And if he took 37 hours to paint the house, he would paint $\frac{1}{37}$ of the house in 1 hour. **So, if he takes A hours to paint the house, he will paint $\frac{1}{A}$ of the house in 1 hour.**

Similarly, if Otto takes $A - 3$ hours to paint the house, he will paint $\frac{1}{A-3}$ of the house in 1 hour. If it takes $A - 8\frac{1}{3}$ hours for both of them working together to paint the house, then they will finish $\frac{1}{A-8\frac{1}{3}}$ of the job in 1 hour. Algebraically, $\frac{1}{A-8\frac{1}{3}}$ simplifies to $\frac{3}{3A-25}$.

So we can now define all six of our quantities:

A = time taken by Adam working alone

$A - 3$ = time taken by Otto working alone

$A - 8\frac{1}{3}$ = time taken by Adam and Otto working together

$\frac{1}{A}$ = amount of the job done by Adam in 1 hour

$\frac{1}{A-3}$ = amount of the job done by Otto in 1 hour

$\frac{3}{3A-25}$ = amount of the job done in 1 hour by Adam and Otto working together

And now we will be ready to set up the equation and solve the problem (which we'll do later).

The area of a rectangle is 108 square feet. If the length is increased by 1 and the width is decreased by 1, the area will be 104 square feet. What are the dimensions of the rectangle?

Originally, on page 21, we set up the variables this way:

First rectangle: Second rectangle:

$A = 108$ $A = 104$
$l = x$ $l = z$
$w = y$ $w = v$

However, the problem tells us that the second rectangle is what we get when we increase the length of the first rectangle by 1, and decrease the width of the first rectangle by 1. In other words, the length of the second rectangle is 1 more than the length of the first, or $x + 1$. Similarly, the width of the second rectangle is 1 less than the width of the first; so the width of the second rectangle is $y - 1$. These two facts reduce the number of variables to two:

First rectangle: Second rectangle:

$A = 108$ $A = 104$
$l = x$ $l = x + 1$
$w = y$ $w = y - 1$

At this point, we have a choice: We can stick with the two variables, and get two equations by using the area formula on both rectangles. Our equations will be $108 = xy$ and $104 = (x + 1)(y - 1)$. If we prefer to reduce to one variable, we can notice that the formula $A = lw$ can be solved for w to give $w = \frac{A}{l}$. Applying that new formula to the first rectangle gives us $y = \frac{108}{x}$. We then use that fact to reduce the number of variables to one:

First rectangle: Second rectangle:

$A = 108$ $A = 104$
$l = x$ $l = x + 1$
$w = \frac{108}{x}$ $w = \frac{108}{x} - 1$

Bob Gorkle left for a bicycle trip at 8:00 AM, cycling at 12 mph. Penny Jarkle followed Bob 30 minutes later, leaving from the same point, and caught up with him at 10:30 AM. How fast was Penny going?

When we looked at this problem before, on page 22, we set up the quantities this way:

Bob's trip: Penny's trip:

$r = 12$ $r = y$
$t = 2.5$ $t = 2$
$d = x$ $d = x$

(See page 22 for an explanation of how we came up with this!)

So far, we have only two variables, x and y, but we would like to reduce that to only one. That turns out to be easy in this case, because the formula $rt = d$, applied to Bob's trip, tells us exactly what d (and therefore x) is: $12(2.5) = 30$. So now we can drop x entirely, and describe everything in terms of numbers and y:

Bob's trip: Penny's trip:

$r = 12$ $r = y$
$t = 2.5$ $t = 2$
$d = 30$ $d = 30$

And, of course, we will now be able to solve the problem easily by applying the formula $rt = d$ to Penny's trip.

An Internet service provider finds that 5000 people will subscribe to its service if the charge is $35 per month. They estimate that for each $1 reduction in the monthly fee, an additional 600 people will sign up. What price should they charge in order to get $257,600 in monthly revenue?

When we looked at this problem in the section on defining variables, we realized that we could use the intermediate variable D to represent the number of $1 reductions in the fee from $35. Our variables were:

S = number of subscribers
F = monthly fee
D = number of $1 reductions from the original $35 fee

Now we want to reduce the number of variables. As we said earlier, if we know the value of D, we can figure out the values of S and F. But we need a translation to an algebraic expression.

If $D = 3$, then what are S and F? Well, S starts with a base of 5,000 and goes up by 600 for each $1 decrease in the fee. So if $D = 3$, then $S = 5,000 + (3 \times 600) = 6,800$. In other words, we added 5,000 plus 600 times D. Therefore, $S = 5,000 + 600D$.

Calculating F when $D = 3$ is easy. $D = 3$ just means there have been 3 $1 decreases from the original fee of $35. When $D = 3$, F must be $35 - 3 = 32$. In other words, we just subtract D from 35, and we get the equation $F = 35 - D$.

Putting it together:

D = number of $1 reductions from the original $35 fee
$S = 5,000 + 600D$
$F = 35 - D$

And therefore, we can define our three quantities this way:

D = number of reductions from the original $35 fee
$5000 + 600D$ = number of subscribers
$35 - D$ = fee

And once again, everything is expressed in terms of one variable.

Final Thoughts on Setting Up Variables

Reading through Chapters 2 and 3, on defining quantities and reducing the number of variables, may have given the reader the idea that the process is long and complex. In most cases, that isn't true. These two chapters have tried to identify the ideas and the logic which may have escaped you when trying to set up word problems. Therefore we have gone into very fine detail in explaining things. Most people, once they become accomplished at doing story problems, do *not* do the definition of quantities and the reducing of the number of variables as two separate steps. For example, let's look at another age problem:

Julius is 23 years older than Augustus. In 25 years, Augustus will be two-thirds of Julius's age. How old are they now?

If you follow the steps discussed in this book so far, you will first set up four variables:

A = Augustus's age now
J = Julius's age now
B = Augustus's age 25 years from now
K = Julius's age 25 years from now

Then you will look at the information in the problem and realize that Augustus's age 25 years from now will be $A + 25$, and similarly Julius's age will be $J + 25$. So we have:

A = Augustus's age now
J = Julius's age now
$A + 25$ = Augustus's age 25 years from now
$J + 25$ = Julius's age 25 years from now

Last of all, you will see that since Julius is 23 years older than Augustus, we can replace J with $A + 23$. And now the quantities are:

A = Augustus's age now
$A + 23$ = Julius's age now
$A + 25$ = Augustus's age 25 years from now
$A + 48$ = Julius's age 25 years from now (simplified from $A + 23 + 25$)

However, after you are experienced with this type of problem, you will be able to go directly to the last set up of quantities without going through the previous steps. It is certainly not wrong to do it that way. In fact it's much better—**if** you can do it reliably and accurately. But the only way you're ever going to be able to do it that fast way, reliably and accurately, is to understand the principles and the steps outlined in Chapter 1 and Chapter 2. So if you find yourself confused or floundering when you try to set up a story problem, go back and do it the slow way, step by step.

Exercise

1. If x stands for an unknown number, what expression stands for 7 more than the unknown number?

2. If x stands for an unknown number, what expression stands for the unknown number less than 7?

3. If x stands for an unknown number, what expression stands for the quotient of 7 and the unknown number?

4. If x stands for an unknown number, what expression stands for the product of 8 and 2 less than the unknown number?

5. If Brenda is x inches tall and Stephanie is 11 inches taller, what stands for Stephanie's height?

In the remaining problems, define all the unknown quantities in terms of one variable. Do not try to solve the problems!

6. Twelve adults are in an elevator. The average weight of the men is 180 pounds and the average weight of the women is 145 pounds. Together they all weigh 1,810 pounds. How many men are there and how many women are there?

7. Dennis can load $\frac{1}{5}$ of a truckful of furniture in 1 hour. When Scott helps him, they get the entire truck loaded in 3 hours. How long does it take Scott to load the truck alone?

8. Marsha is 15 years younger than Karen. Twelve years ago, Karen was four times Marsha's age. How long ago was Karen twice Marsha's age?

9. A two-digit number is one less than twice the number obtained when the digits are reversed. The sum of the two digits is 10. What is the number?

10. The cost of 12 calculators is $175.89 more than the cost of one calculator. How much does one calculator cost?

11. The ratio of men to women in a nursing class is 2:3. There are 35 people in the class. How many are women?

12. A straight road runs from West Haircut through Middle Haircut to East Haircut. The distance from West Haircut to East Haircut is 190 miles. Middle Haircut is 1.5 times as far from East Haircut as it is from West Haircut. How far is it from East Haircut to Middle Haircut?

13. The Swinging Chess Club has an annual membership fee of $35.00, and 2 members. The management of the club figures that they would get 10 additional members for each dollar reduction in the annual fee. What should they charge in order to collect $2,214 in membership fees?

14. Mr. & Mrs. Globulin's property taxes increased by 15% this year. Their total property taxes last year and this year combined were $1,444.80. How much did they pay last year?

15. Three consecutive odd integers add up to 759. What are the integers?

16. How much plain water should be added to 65 gallons of a 24% okra juice solution in order to obtain a 1% solution?

SETTING UP AND SOLVING THE EQUATIONS

Finally we are ready to talk about solving the problems. The reader should keep in mind, however, that the skills of defining quantities and reducing the number of variables **must** be mastered before there is any chance of setting up the equations properly! It was not by accident that we spent so much time and space on those two steps. The heart of solving word problems is the precise, complete, and accurate definition of quantities, **not** the setting up of equations. For most cases in this chapter, we will find that the equation or equations are very easy to set up once we have defined our quantities correctly.

The Word "Is"

Just as the word "it" is the nastiest word in solving story problems, the word "is" is probably the nicest. Very often, the word "is" translates directly into an equal sign.

EXAMPLE

The first of two numbers is 18 larger than the second. Twice the first number is 15 more than three times the second. Find the two numbers.

Using the ideas already discussed in this book, we set up our quantities this way:

> y = the *second* number
> $y + 18$ = the *first* number
> $2(y + 18)$ = twice the first number
> $3y$ = three times the second number

Now we look at the information in the problem. There are two sentences which contain the word "is." Which one shall we use to set up our equation? The answer is very important. **We use the information which has not yet been used to set up the variable quantities.** When we decided that y would be the second number and that $y + 18$ would be the first, we used all the information we could get from the first sentence in the problem statement. *We cannot use the same information again to set up the equation.* If we *did* make this mistake, here is what would happen:

Translating "The first of two numbers is 18 larger than the second" into an equation, we have:

$$y + 18 = y + 18$$

That's right, isn't it? The left-hand side is what we have already set up for "the first number," and the right-hand side is 18 more than the second number (which is y). Obviously, we will get nothing useful from our equation here, because $y + 18$ always equals $y + 18$, no matter what y is.

What we *should* do is to use the second sentence, because it contains information we haven't used yet: namely, that twice the first number is 15 more than three times the second. We have set up expressions to represent twice the first number and three times the second, but there is nothing in our setup which says that one of those is 15 more than the other. So now we will translate the sentence "twice the first number is 15 more than three times the second" into an equation:

$$2(y + 18) = 15 + 3y$$

This is exactly what we want. Note that the left-hand side is twice the first number, and that the right-hand side is 15 plus three times the second number.

Solving the equation, we get $y = 21$. That is not quite the whole story, of course. The problem asked for *both* numbers. A look at how we set up our quantities will tell us that y was supposed to stand for the second number, and that the first number was $y + 18$. Therefore the first number is 39, and the second is 21.

Variations of "Is"

Sometimes the "equals" comes from a different form of "is," such as "was" or "will be."

EXAMPLE

Mary is 7 years older than Jill. Two years ago, she was twice as old as Jill is now. How old are Mary and Jill?

Using our knowledge of how to set up variables and expressions, we get:

J = Jill's age
$J + 7$ = Mary's age
$J + 5$ = Mary's age two years ago (simplified from $J + 7 - 2$)

Once again, we have already used all the information in the first sentence of the problem statement. So we will set up our equation using the second sentence. If we don't see immediately how to set the equation up from that sentence, we can rewrite it to refer explicitly to the quantities we have identified:

Mary's age two years ago was two times Jill's [present] age.

Now we see that the word "was" will translate into an equal sign, and the words on either side of the word "was" refer directly to our defined quantities:

$$J + 5 = 2J$$

This equation is simple to solve, of course, and we get $J = 5$. So you have the problem right if you put "5" in the answer blank on your test, right?

WRONG!!! The problem asked for Mary's age *and* Jill's age. To answer the problem fully, we must say "Jill is 5, and Mary is 12." (Mary is 12 because Mary's age is $J + 7$, which equals 12.)

Exercise

Define the quantities, and then solve the following problem:

The sum of three consecutive odd integers is 111. Find the three integers.

Exercise

Using the quantities defined in the previous chapters, construct an equation for the following problem, and solve it:

The sum of the digits of a two-digit number is 11. If the digits are reversed, the new number will be 45 less than the original. What is the number?

  Using Information Not Used in Defining Variable Quantities

The equation or equations in a story problem are generally going to use information which was not used in defining the variable quantities. Let's look at a previous example, this time paying close attention to the information not used for the variables.

EXAMPLE

Otto Biography can paint a particular house in 3 hours less than Adam Bomb can paint it. Working together, they can paint the house in $5\frac{1}{3}$ hours less than it takes Otto. How long does it take Adam to paint the house?

We have defined the quantities in Chapter 3, page 45:

A = time taken by Adam working alone

$A - 3$ = time taken by Otto working alone

$A - 8\frac{1}{3}$ = time taken by Adam and Otto working together

$\frac{1}{A}$ = amount of the job done by Adam in 1 hour

$\frac{1}{A-3}$ = amount of the job done by Otto in 1 hour

$\frac{3}{3A-25}$ = amount of the job done in 1 hour by Adam and Otto working together

We are now ready to use the expressions above to set up an equation. Unfortunately, there is nothing in the problem statement which says that one quantity "is" the same as some other quantity, so we will have to figure out the equation for ourselves. Looking at the problem statement and at the definitions of the quantities, we see that we have already used the fact that Otto's time is 3 hours less than Adam's, and that their time when working together is $5\frac{1}{3}$ hours less than Otto's. What we *haven't* used is this:

The amount of the job done in 1 hour when working together is the amount of the job done by Otto in 1 hour when working alone, plus the amount done by Adam in 1 hour when working alone.

Please read the sentence above as many times as you need to, until you understand it. That sentence is the key to all "Adam can do a job in 7 hours..."-type problems. When we defined the amount of the job Adam and Otto do together in 1 hour as $\frac{3}{3A-25}$, we were using the fact that the time it takes Adam and Otto to do the job together is $A - 8\frac{1}{3}$. We get the amount of work done together by adding together the amounts of work done by Adam and Otto separately.

Notice once more that it is not correct to add together the times it takes Adam and Otto to do the job separately. That would make no sense at all. If we added Otto's time plus Adam's time, we would have the time it would take Otto to do the job alone, and then for Adam to arrive and do the job himself all over again. That makes no sense, and it has no relevance to the problem. However, adding together the *work* that each person does makes perfect sense, and that is what the **bold** sentence above tells us.

So now let's translate the **bold** sentence to an equation:

$$\frac{3}{3A-25} = \frac{1}{A-3} + \frac{1}{A}$$

This is exactly right, because the left-hand side is the amount done by both men together in 1 hour, and the right-hand side is the amount done by Adam in one hour plus the amount done by Otto in one hour.

This equation has two solutions: $\frac{5}{3}$, and 15. We notice first that the two solutions ARE NOT THE TWO TIMES FOR ADAM AND OTTO!!! How do we know? Because the letter A stands for Adam's time, and nothing else!

Are there, then, two possible solutions to this problem, one in which Adam paints the house in 15 hours and the other in which he paints it in $\frac{5}{3}$ hours? Well, that is theoretically possible, and we have to consider all mathematically correct possibilities. But in this case, the answer of $\frac{5}{3}$ makes no sense. Why? This is another application of "Common Sense." We already know that Otto can paint the house 3 hours quicker than Adam can paint it. So if Adam paints the house in $\frac{5}{3}$ hours, then Otto paints it in $\frac{5}{3} - 3 = -\frac{4}{3}$ hours. It is unlikely that even the most efficient painter can paint the house in a negative amount of time! Therefore we must discard the answer which says $A = \frac{5}{3}$.

Can we then say that 15 hours is the answer to the problem? *Yes*, because the problem asked us for the length of time it takes Adam to paint the house. Looking at our definitions of quantities, we see that A stands for exactly what we were asked for, and so we are finished as soon as we have discovered the value of A.

Another example is in order to further help illustrate how to use unused information once the variables have been established.

EXAMPLE

A Cadillac costs $9,400 more than a Chevrolet. Three Chevrolets cost the same as two Cadillacs. How much does each car cost?

When we looked at this problem in Chapter 2, page 15, we rewrote it like this:

> *The price of a Cadillac is $9400 more than the price of a Chevrolet. Three times the price of a Chevrolet is the same as two times the price of a Cadillac. What is the price of each car?*

We already know that we can set up the quantities like this, using only one variable:

x = price of a Chevrolet
$x + 9,400$ = price of a Cadillac

We have already used the information that a Cadillac is $9,400 more expensive than a Chevrolet. To set up an equation, we must use additional, unused information. The additional, unused information indicates that three times the price of a Chevrolet is the same as two times the price of a Cadillac. So our equation is this:

$3x = 2(x + 9,400)$

The $3x$ stands for "three times the price of a Chevrolet," the equal sign stands for "is the same as," and the $2(x + 9,400)$ stands for "two times the price of a Cadillac."

The solution to the equation is $x = 18,800$. So what is the answer to the problem? Review the definitions of our quantities, and we see that x stood for the price of a Chevrolet. We look at the statement of the problem, and we see that we were asked for the prices of both a Chevrolet and a Cadillac. So the 18,800 is **part** of the answer. The other part of the answer is the price of a Cadillac. The definitions of the quantities tell us that the price of a Cadillac is $x + 9,400$, which is $18,800 + 9,400 = 28,200$. So the solution to the problem is:

> price of a Chevrolet = $18,800
> price of a Cadillac = $28,200

When the Same Quantity Can Be Expressed in Two Ways

Let's revisit this problem from Chapter 2, page 19:

EXAMPLE

A chemical manufacturer wants to mix some 10% pesticide solution with 500 gallons of a 2% pesticide solution, so that the resulting mixture is a 4.5% pesticide solution. How much of the 10% pesticide solution should be used?

Using the ideas we have already learned, we set up our quantities as follows:

> x = amount in gallons of 10% pesticide solution used
> 500 = amount of 2% pesticide solution used
> $.1x$ = amount of pure pesticide in the 10% solution used
> $.02(500) = 10$ = amount of pure pesticide in the 2% solution used
> $500 + x$ = amount of mixed solution
> $.045(500 + x)$ = total pure pesticide in the mixed solution

Some readers who are paying close attention, and thinking carefully, might notice this: We could have defined the last quantity, the total amount of pure pesticide in the mixed solution, in a completely different way. We could have simply added the pure pesticide from the 10% solution, plus the pure pesticide from the 2% solution. In that case, we would have said:

> $.1x + 10$ = total pure pesticide in the mixed solution.

So which way is right? The answer is that *both* are right, and in fact knowing that both are right gives us the equation we want! A very important principle is at work here, one which is worth stating separately:

If any quantity can be represented by two different algebraic expressions, then those two expressions are equal to each other.

The fact stated above is, like all mathematics, carefully applied common sense. Obviously, if we could calculate the amount of pure pesticide either by $.1x + 10$ or by $.045(500 + x)$, we had better get the same answer either way, right? The only way for this to happen is for the two expressions to be equal to each other.

So, our equation is:

$$.1x + 10 = .045(500 + x)$$

Solving for x, we get $\frac{2500}{11}$, or $227\frac{3}{11}$, or 227.3 gallons. Now we check to see what x was supposed to stand for, and what quantity the problem asked for. It turns out that x stands for the amount of 10% pesticide solution to be used, which was the quantity the problem asked for, and so we are finished. The answer is 227.3 gallons.

Equations Which Come from Geometric Facts and Formulas

Sometimes the equation in a story problem doesn't come from given information, but rather from geometric facts which you are expected to know.

Facts

The largest of three angles in a triangle is 109° larger than the smallest angle. The angle in the middle is 46° more than three times the smallest. What are the angles?

Setting up the quantities is straightforward:

x = smallest angle
$x + 109$ = largest angle
$46 + 3x$ = middle angle

But where do we get an equation? We have already used all the information given in the problem when we set up the quantities. The writer of the problem expected you to know that the three angles in any triangle always add up to 180°. If you didn't know that, you would have no hope of solving the problem. *That* fact (that the three angles add up to 180°) is going to give us our equation:

$$x + (x + 109) + (46 + 3x) = 180$$

And the solution is $x = 5$. So what is the solution to the problem? The problem asked for all three angles. The letter x stands for the smallest angle. The largest angle is $x + 109° = 114°$, and the middle angle is $3x + 46° = 61°$ (see how nice it is, and even necessary, to write down exactly the expression that stands for each quantity?). Therefore the three angles are 5°, 114°, and 61°.

 Using Formulas

The simple interest on an account over a period of 2 years was $89.70. The account paid annual interest at the rate of 5.75%. How much was originally in the account?

When we discussed this problem in Chapter 2, page 20, we mentioned that the formula for simple interest is $I = Prt$. For the variables, we came up with:

> $I = 89.70$
> $P =$ unknown
> $r = .0575$
> $t = 2$

In this problem, there is only one period of time, with a constant rate of interest and principal. Also, we have set up the variables in the formula so that there is only one unknown. Under those conditions, we can use the formula just once to solve the problem:

> $89.70 = P(.0575)(2)$

And the solution is $P = \$780.00$.

 Using Formulas Twice

The area of a rectangle is 108 square feet. If the length is increased by 1 and the width is decreased by 1, the area will be 104 square feet. What are the dimensions of the rectangle?

When we discussed this problem in the previous chapter, on page 46, we set up the following:

First rectangle:	Second rectangle:
$A = 108$	$A = 104$
$l = x$	$l = x + 1$
$w = y$	$w = y - 1$

Since the area of each rectangle is defined by the formula $A = lw$, we get two equations from the two rectangles:

> $108 = xy$ [first rectangle]
> $104 = (x + 1)(y - 1)$ [second rectangle]

Solving those two equations simultaneously, we get two solutions: One solution is $x = 12$ and $y = 9$, and the other is $x = -9$ and $y = -12$. However, x and y stand for the length and width of a rectangle, and it makes no sense to have negative lengths and widths. So we discard the solution $x = -9$, $y = -12$. Once again, we look back at the statement of the problem to find out exactly what quantities were asked for, and we look at the definitions of the variables to make sure we can identify those same quantities. In this case, we are asked for the dimensions of the original (first) rectangle. That's exactly what x and y are: x is the length, and y is the width. So we have our solution: length = 12, and width = 9.

Here is another example to illustrate how a formula is used twice.

An airplane whose speed in still air is 250 mph flies against a headwind for 3 hours, and then turns around and returns with the wind. The airplane's total trip takes 5 hours and 15 minutes. How fast was the wind blowing, and how far did the plane travel on its round trip?

This problem was Exercise J in the previous chapter. At that time, it was specified that W would be used to stand for the speed of the wind.

There are actually two trips in this problem: The trip against the wind and the trip with the wind. We know we need to describe the two trips separately, because the speed of the plane (with respect to the ground) was not the same for both trips. The formula $rt = d$ applies only when the speed is constant. So we set up our r, t, and d for each trip:

Against the wind:

$r = 250 - W$

$t = 3$

$d = d$

With the wind:

$r = 250 + W$

$t = 5\frac{1}{4} - 3 = 2\frac{1}{4} = \frac{9}{4}$

$d = d$

We used d for the distance in both trips, since the distance going out is obviously the same as the distance returning. We got the $t = \frac{9}{4}$ for the second trip by subtracting the total time minus the time for the first trip.

Now we have two equations with two unknowns:

$(250 - W)3 = d$ $\qquad$ $(250 + W)\frac{9}{4} = d$

The solution to this system of equations is $W = \frac{250}{7}$, or about 35.71, and $d = \frac{4500}{7}$, or about 642.86.

The problem asked for the speed of the wind and the *total* distance traveled by the plane. The speed of the wind was designated by W, so the answer is 35.71 mph. The total distance traveled by the plane was the total of the *two* distances on the two legs of the trip. Both of those distances were 642.86, so the total distance is 2 × 642.86, or about 1285.7 miles.

 Variation Problems

Variation problems are a special case which uses more than one occurence of the same formula.

The amount of medication to be administered to a patient varies directly with the patient's weight. If the dosage for a 100-lb. person is 3 mg., then how much should be given to a 175-lb. person?

When we discussed this problem in the chapter on Defining Quantities, on pages 22-23, we set up the following values for two occurrences of the formula $Q_1 = Q_2 k$:

First occurrence:

$$Q_1 = 3$$
$$Q_2 = 100$$
$$k = \text{unknown (we can use the letter } k \text{ in both occurrences because it will be the same value both times)}$$

Second occurrence:

$$Q_1 = x \text{ (unknown)}$$
$$Q_2 = 175$$
$$k = k \text{ (same value as in the first occurrence above)}$$

Making the proper substitutions for the first occurrence of the formula, we get

$$3 = 100k$$

to which the solution is $k = .03$. Using that value along with $Q_2 = 175$ for the second occurrence, we get

$$x = 175(.03)$$

and the solution is 5.25. Since x stood for Q_1, which was the amount of medication required, and since that is the quantity the problem asked for, our solution is 5.25 mg.

Exercise

Using the previous example as a model, solve the following problem. Refer back to Chapter 2, pages 23-24 (where this problem was discussed), if necessary.

The number of phone calls between two cities each business day varies jointly with the populations of the two cities, and inversely with the square of the distance between the cities. Dweebville has a population of 10,000. Dork Springs, 25 miles away, has a population of 20,000. There are approximately 8,000 calls each business day between the two cities. About how many calls per day will there be between Kansas City (population 435,000) and St. Louis (population 397,000), 260 miles apart?

Exponential Growth and Decay

Exponential growth and decay problems are also a special case which uses more than one occurrence of the same formula.

In 1910 the population of Kentucky was 2.28 million. In 1940 the population was 2.85 million. If the population continued to grow at the same constant rate that it averaged from 1910 to 1940, what should the population have been in 1990?

When we dealt with this problem earlier in Chapter 2, pages 25-27, we stated that we would use the exponential growth formula, $Q = Q_0 e^{kt}$, twice, with the following substitutions:

First period (1910 to 1940):

$Q = 2.85$ million
$Q_0 = 2.28$ million
$k = $ unknown
$t = 30$

Second period (1940 to 1990):

$Q = x$ (unknown)
$Q_0 = 2.85$ million
$k = $ unknown
$t = 50$

When we set up the first occurrence of the formula, we get

$$2.85 = 2.28\, e^{30k}$$

Solving for k, we get $k = 0.0074381$ **(Advice: when you solve for k and then use the value for k in another equation, use all the decimal places for k instead of rounding off. A tiny difference in**

61

k can make a big difference in your final answer.) We can now use the value 0.0074381 for k in the second occurrence of the formula:

$$x = 2.85e^{(0.0074381)(50)}$$

Solving for x, we get 4.1339 (million). Looking back at the problem and the definitions of the quantities, we see that x stands for exactly what we were asked for. The answer to the problem is 4.1339 million. (By the way, the actual population of Kentucky in 1990 was only 3.69 million, which means the rate of growth must have been slower from 1940 to 1990 than it had been from 1910 to 1940.)

Percent Problems

There is (sort of) a formula for translating percent problems into an equation. If we have set up the percent, the base, and the percent quantity, all in terms of one variable, then we can translate into the following equation:

$$\frac{\textbf{percent}}{100} = \frac{\textbf{percent quantity}}{\textbf{base}}$$

Baseball player Steve Orino got hits in 23 out of 89 official at bats. What percent of his at bats were hits?

We have already decided (see page 25) that the quantities here are:

x = percent (unknown)
89 = at bats (base)
23 = hits (percent quantity)

Translating the **bold** equation above, we get

$$\frac{x}{100} = \frac{23}{89}$$

The solution is $x = 25.8$. We made x stand for the percent, and the percent is what the problem asked for. The solution is 25.8%.

Percent Increases and Decreases

The price of a new car has been reduced by 7%. The new price is $20,088. What was the original price?

When we dealt with this problem before, on page 37, we came up with the following definitions of the quantities:

P = original price of the car (the base)
7 = percent
$P - 20,088$ = amount of decrease (also the percent quantity)

Using the pattern for percent equations, we translate this to:

$$\frac{7}{100} = \frac{P-20{,}088}{P}$$

and the solution is $P = 21{,}600$. Since P stands for the original price, and the original price is what the problem asked for, the answer to the problem is $21,600.

Note: It would also be correct to notice that we could have expressed the amount of decrease as 7% of P, or $.07P$. Then we would have used the principle that if the same quantity can be represented by two different expressions, then those two expressions are equal to each other. That would have given us the equation:

$$.07P = P - 20{,}088$$

The solution to that equation, also, is $P = 21{,}600$.

 Ratios

We look again at this problem:

The ratio of men to women in Professor Shockem's electrical engineering class is $1\frac{1}{2}$ times the ratio of men to women in Professor Tinear's music class. If there are 12 men and 12 women in the electrical engineering class, and a total of 35 students in the music class, how many men and how many women are in the music class?

In the previous chapter, on page 44, we set up the quantities this way:

men in electrical engineering class = 12
women in electrical engineering class = 12
ratio of men to women in electrical engineering class = $\frac{12}{12} = 1$
men in music class = M
women in music class = $35 - M$
ratio of men to women in music class = $\frac{M}{35-M}$

Now that the quantities are defined, it is an easy matter to set up the equation. The problem presents us with the word "is," exactly where it needs to be to define an equation. "The ratio of men to women in Professor Shockem's electrical engineering class **is** $1\frac{1}{2}$ times the ratio of men to women in Professor Tinear's music class." We did not use that information while setting up the variables and expressions. And a close reading of the rest of the problem will show that we did use every other piece of information to set up the quantities. Therefore, the equation we want is:

$$1 = 1\tfrac{1}{2} \times \frac{M}{35-M}$$

The solution is $M = 14$. The problem asked for the number of men and the number of women in the music class. The number of men, M, is therefore 14. The number of women, $35 - M$, is therefore 21.

Ratios are sometimes hard to recognize. A common use of the ratio idea is a problem like the following:

A forest management team caught 82 trout in a lake, tagged them all, and put them back into the lake. Two weeks later, they caught 110 trout, and found that 23 of them were tagged. About how many trout are in the lake?

This problem is unusual in that the quantities are quite easy to identify, but it is not obvious what to do with them. Even here, however, it is the hidden meaning of one of the quantities which gives us the key:

> x = number of trout in the lake
> 82 = number caught and tagged first time
> 110 = number caught second time
> 23 = number of the second batch which were tagged

This is all we need for setting up the variables, but where is the ratio? One thing we might try is to assume that the ratio of tagged trout to total trout is the same for both fishing expeditions. But that obviously isn't true: The ratio of tagged trout to total trout in the second trip was $\frac{23}{110}$; but on the first trip, *all* the trout ended up being tagged. The ratio was $\frac{82}{82}$!

The answer becomes clearer if we look again at that first quantity, 82. We called it "number caught and tagged first time," and that's true. But the 82 represents something more significant than that: *82 is the total number of tagged trout in the lake.* (We are assuming, of course, that there were no tagged trout in the lake before this experiment was carried out.) Now let's look at the quantities again:

> x = number of trout in the lake
> 82 = number of tagged trout in the lake
> 110 = number caught second time
> 23 = number of the second batch which were tagged

Now we can think of a logical proportion: The ratio of total trout in the lake to tagged trout in the lake is probably about the same as the ratio of total trout to tagged trout in the second catch. And that will give us a perfectly respectable equation:

$$\frac{x}{82} = \frac{110}{23}$$

The solution is $x = 392.17$, and x represents the total number of trout in the lake. So we estimate the trout population of the lake to be about 392.

UNITS

Read the following problem:

Jill is 4 inches taller than Deborah. Together their heights add up to 11 feet. How tall is each woman?

A student set up the problem this way:

D = Deborah's height
$D + 4$ = Jill's height

and then wrote the following equation:

$D + (D + 4) = 11$

What was the student's mistake?

The mistake is that the expression on the left-hand side of the equation refers to *inches*, but the number on the right-hand side refers to *feet*. We cannot set feet equal to inches!

We can avoid this mistake by specifying the units we are using to measure or count our quantities whenever we define variables in a problem which uses more than one unit for measuring the same thing. "Using more than one unit for measuring the same thing" means things like:

Length measured in feet for some quantities and in miles for others.
Money calculated in cents for some quantities and in dollars for others.
Time measured in days for some quantities and in hours for others.

In the problem above, the student should have set up the variables this way:

D = Deborah's height in inches
$D + 4$ = Jill's height in inches

Then, when the equation is set up, the student will be more likely to recognize that you can't have inches equal to feet.

The correct equation will then be $D + (D + 4) = 132$. Shortly, we will discuss conversion of units in detail. For now, the point to remember is that whenever more than one unit of measurement is used in a problem, the definition of variables should include the units in which the quantity is measured.

Define the unknown quantities in this problem:

Ramon takes 20 minutes longer than Carlos to type a document. Working together, then can have the entire document typed in 3 hours. How long does it take each of them, working alone, to type it?

Perhaps the most common error in dealing with units comes with coin problems. We have already seen the following problem in Chapters 2 and 3:

Jenny's coin purse contains 28 coins, all nickels and quarters. The total value of the coins is $2.40. How many of each kind does she have?

Many people will conscientiously define their variables this way:

N = number of nickels
$28 - N$ = number of quarters
$5N$ = total value of the nickels
$25(28 - N)$ = total value of the quarters

which is entirely correct, **if they keep in mind that the total value of quarters and nickels is being expressed in cents**. But if they then set up the following equation:

$5N + 25(28 - N) = 2.40$

they will get the problem wrong. That's because the right-hand side of the equation refers to dollars, but the left-hand side refers to cents!

In a problem such as this one, whether you choose to work in dollars or cents is a matter of taste. Most people probably prefer to use cents, because it avoids decimal points. In this particular problem, if we decide to use cents, then the total value of all the coins should be written as 240¢, not as $2.40. On the other hand, if we decide to use dollars, then the total value of the nickels would be .05N instead of $5N$, and the total value of the quarters would be .25(28 − N) instead of 25(28 − N).

Conversion of Units

Many people have trouble converting, for example, feet to inches, because they can't remember whether to multiply by 12 or divide by 12. The concept of unit fractions can help avoid this trouble.

A unit fraction is a fraction whose numerator is equal to its denominator, but whose numerator and denominator are expressed in different units. For example, the following are unit fractions:

$$\frac{12 \text{ inches}}{1 \text{ foot}} \qquad \frac{1 \text{ hour}}{60 \text{ minutes}} \qquad \frac{4 \text{ quarts}}{1 \text{ gallon}} \qquad \frac{1 \text{ kilogram}}{2.2 \text{ pounds}}$$

$$\frac{1 \text{ foot}}{12 \text{ inches}} \qquad \frac{60 \text{ minutes}}{1 \text{ hour}} \qquad \frac{1 \text{ gallon}}{4 \text{ quarts}} \qquad \frac{2.2 \text{ pounds}}{1 \text{ kilogram}}$$

Unit fractions are useful because they are all equal to 1. That's because the numerator is always equal to the denominator. And, when we multiply any quantity by 1, we don't change the value of the quantity. So look what happens when we multiply 17 feet by a unit fraction:

$$(17 \text{ feet}) \times \frac{12 \text{ inches}}{1 \text{ foot}} = \left(\frac{17 \text{ feet}}{1}\right) \times \frac{12 \text{ inches}}{1 \text{ foot}} = \frac{204 \text{ inches}}{1} = 204 \text{ inches}$$

It may look suspicious to cancel the word "feet" (especially since the denominator of the second fraction actually had the word "foot" instead of "feet"). But it's actually perfectly legal, and it works! The fact is that 17 feet is equal to 204 inches.

The procedure for using unit fractions to convert units is this: Form a unit fraction in which the denominator is expressed in the units you want to get rid of, and the numerator is expressed in the new units you want to use. Then multiply your original value by that unit fraction, canceling units from top and bottom where possible.

EXAMPLE

Convert 298 minutes to hours.

SOLUTION:

We need a unit fraction where the denominator is expressed in minutes (because we want to get rid of the minutes) and the numerator is expressed in hours. Since 1 hour and 60 minutes are the same length of time, the unit fraction we want is $\frac{1 \text{ hour}}{60 \text{ minutes}}$. Now we multiply:

$$\frac{298 \text{ minutes}}{1} \times \frac{1 \text{ hour}}{60 \text{ minutes}} = \frac{298 \text{ hours}}{60} = \frac{298}{60} \text{ hours} = 4.97 \text{ hours}$$

Sometimes we need to go through two or more multiplications of unit fractions because we don't know an equivalence between the two units we are dealing with.

EXAMPLE

Convert 6,800 feet to kilometers.

SOLUTION:

We might not know how many feet are in a kilometer. But if we know the number of inches in a foot, the number of inches in a meter, and the number of meters in a kilometer, we can do the job:

$$\frac{6800 \text{ feet}}{1} \times \frac{12 \text{ inches}}{1 \text{ foot}} \times \frac{1 \text{ meter}}{39.37 \text{ inches}} \times \frac{1 \text{ kilometer}}{1000 \text{ meters}}$$

$$= \frac{6800 \times 12}{39.37 \times 1000} \text{ kilometers}$$

$$= 2.073 \text{ kilometers}$$

Convert 5.6 days to minutes, using unit fractions.

The Word "Per"

Sometimes values are expressed in one unit per some other unit, such as "miles per hour." For purposes of mathematical calculation, we regard such values as fractions, in which the denominator is the unit which follows the word "per."

EXAMPLE

"58 miles per hour" is equal to the fraction $\frac{58\ miles}{1\ hour}$.

Therefore, if we want to convert 58 miles per hour into miles per day, we multiply by a unit fraction which has hours on top (to get rid of the "hour" unit on the bottom of the original number) and days on the bottom:

$$\frac{58\ miles}{1\ hour} \times \frac{24\ hours}{1\ day} = \frac{1392\ miles}{1\ day} = 1{,}392 \text{ miles per day}$$

If we wanted to convert 58 miles per hour to inches per second, we would do this:

$$\frac{58\ miles}{1\ hour} \times \frac{5280\ feet}{1\ mile} \times \frac{12\ inches}{1\ foot} \times \frac{1\ hour}{60\ minutes} \times \frac{1\ minute}{60\ seconds} = \frac{3{,}674{,}880\ inches}{3600\ seconds}$$
$$= 1{,}020.8 \text{ inches per second}$$

Exercise

Convert 2.6 pounds per inch to kilograms per meter.

Tables of equivalent values for building unit fractions can be found in the Appendix, on page 119.

Exercise

1. Convert 10,000 inches per minute to miles per hour.

2. Convert 10,000 days to years.

3. Convert 10,000 square inches to square feet.

4. Convert 10,000 cubic inches to cubic feet.

5. A collection of 68 pennies and quarters is worth $5.00. How many quarters, how many pennies?

6. During a $3\frac{1}{2}$-hour evening, Danny spent 45 minutes more playing Nintendo than he did studying for his algebra test. How much time did he spend on each activity?

7. Kareem is 22 inches taller than Muggsy. Together they are 12 feet 6 inches tall. How tall is each?

8. There are 40 boxes of cookies in a crate. A store accepted a shipment of 4 crates plus 15 boxes. They put $\frac{3}{7}$ of the boxes on the shelf. How many full crates and how many additional boxes were left over?

DIAGRAMS

Diagrams have perhaps been overemphasized as a tool for solving word problems in algebra. The fact is, in most algebraic word problems there aren't any diagrams which can be of help. However, in cases where diagrams are appropriate, they can be helpful. This Chapter will give examples of problems in which diagrams can help to clarify the quantities and their relationships.

EXAMPLES

○ *The perimeter of a rectangle is 50 cm. and the area of the same rectangle is 126 cm². Find the dimensions of the rectangle.*

SOLUTION:

Some students might find it unnecessary to draw a diagram for this problem, but others might understand the problem better if they had a picture of what's being asked. Since we don't know the length or the width of the rectangle, we must label those dimensions with letters:

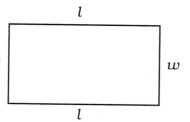

One advantage of the diagram is that, even if we forget the formula for the perimeter of a rectangle ($P = 2l + 2w$), we might be able to reason it out from looking at the diagram. As we walk around the rectangle, let's say, clockwise from the upper left-hand corner, we would first travel along a length, then a width, then a second length, and then a second width. At that point we would be back where we started, at the upper left-hand corner. Reviewing our travels, we see that the perimeter must be $l + w + l + w$, or, more simply, $2l + 2w$.

Once we remember (or figure out) the formulas for the area and perimeter of a rectangle, the equations are obvious:

$$lw = 126$$
$$2l + 2w = 50$$

The solutions are $l = 18$, $w = 7$, and $l = 7$, $w = 18$. (These two are for all practical purposes the same solution.) Traditionally the word "length" is used to describe the longer dimension of the rectangle, so we would probably just say that the length is 18 cm. and the width is 7 cm.

One side of a triangle is 3 inches longer than the second side. The third side is 18 inches less than the sum of the other two sides. The perimeter of the triangle is 40 inches. Find the lengths of the three sides.

SOLUTION:

Once again, it is possible to do this problem without a diagram, but many people are more comfortable with something to look at. For this problem, note that the sides are specifically described as "one side" (which we could call the first side), the "second side," and "the third side."

We could label the three sides as x, y, and z; or we could do some reasoning about the problem before labeling the sides. The first sentence in the problem says "one side of a triangle is 3 inches longer than the second side." That is a comparison between two quantities. We recall, from Chapter 3 Reducing the Number of Variables, that it is usually wise to let a variable stand for the *second* quantity mentioned, and then describe the first quantity in terms of the second. So we will allow x to represent the second side, and then the *first* side will be $x + 3$.

At this point we have a choice of how to label the third side: We could just use another letter, y, or we could use the sentence "the third side is 18 inches less than the sum of the other two sides" in order to get an expression for the third side involving x. If it is going to be a struggle to express that third side in terms of x, we prefer to postpone the struggle until after we have drawn the diagram. So, our diagram will look like that above.

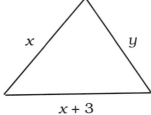

Since we have two unknowns, x and y, we will need two equations. The two equations will be comparatively easy to get, because there are two pieces of information we haven't used yet: The fact that the third side is 18 inches less than the sum of the other two sides, and the fact that the perimeter is 40 inches. [If we don't remember the formula for the perimeter of a triangle, we can figure it out by looking at the diagram, much as we did with the rectangle in the previous example.]

The statement "the third side is 18 inches less than the sum of the other two sides" translates directly into the equation:

$$y = (x + 3) + x - 18 \quad \text{or} \quad y = 2x - 15$$

The statement that the perimeter is 40 inches translates into:

$$(x + 3) + x + y = 40 \quad \text{or} \quad 2x + y + 3 = 40$$

The solution to the two equations is $x = 13$, $y = 11$. Since the problem asked for the lengths of all three sides, we now look back at the diagram and see that the lengths we seek are $x + 3$, x, and y. Those lengths are 16, 13, and 11. So that is the answer, and we're finished.

Drawing a diagram is an obvious strategy in problems such as the two previous, where the entire question is centered around a geometric shape such as a rectangle or triangle. It is not as obvious that a diagram can sometimes help us to solve a rate-time-distance problem, such as the one below.

EXAMPLE

The cities of Dripping Faucet and Stench Lake are 800 miles apart. A train left Dripping Faucet, traveling toward Stench Lake at 70 miles per hour, at 2:00 PM. Another train left Stench Lake, heading for Dripping Faucet at 76 mph, at 3:00 PM. How far from Stench Lake were the trains when they collided? (They were computer-controlled trains with no passengers or engineers aboard. Nobody was hurt.)

SOLUTION:

For the time being, we will draw the diagram with the distance between Stench Lake and the collision point represented by the letter *x*. We will also use the letter *a* to represent the distance from Dripping Faucet to the collision point, since that is the distance the train from Dripping Faucet will cover in its trip. The only other quantity we will show in the diagram is the 800-mile distance between the two cities.

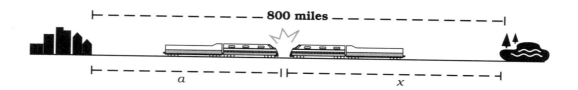

This is a rate-time-distance problem in which there are two separate trips, each with its own rate, time, and distance. We will therefore have two occurrences of the formula $rt = d$, one for each train. Even without the diagram, we could set up our quantities this way:

Train from Dripping Faucet to Stench Lake:

$r = 70$
$t = b$
$d = a$

Train from Stench Lake to Dripping Faucet:

$r = 76$
$t = b - 1$ (this train left 1 hour after the other one, so it had been
        traveling 1 hour less time)
$d = x$

Looking at what we have set up here, we might notice a difficulty. We have three unknown quantities, but we have only two obvious equations. Applying $rt = d$ to the trip from Dripping Faucet to Stench Lake will give us:

$$70b = a$$

And applying $rt = d$ to the other trip will give us:

$$76(b - 1) = x$$

At this point we might look back at the statement of the problem, to see what information we haven't used. We can see that the 800-mile distance between the two cities is not represented anywhere in our equations or in the definitions of the quantities. Even after we've seen that, however, it might not be obvious what to do with that information.

Diagram to the rescue! When we look at the diagram, it is clear that the distances a and x add up to 800 miles. In fact, now that we know that, we don't really need to use a at all. We could represent the distance between Dripping Faucet and the collision point as $800 - x$. So let's go back and redefine the quantities, and then reconstruct the equations:

Train from Dripping Faucet to Stench Lake:

$$r = 70$$
$$t = b$$
$$d = 800 - x$$

Equation: $70b = 800 - x$

Train from Stench Lake to Dripping Faucet:

$$r = 76$$
$$t = b - 1$$
$$d = x$$

Equation: $76(b - 1) = x$

We have two equations in two unknowns, b and x. The solution to the two equations is $x = 380$, $b = 6$. The quantity asked for in the problem was the distance from Stench Lake to the collision point. That quantity was represented by x, and the answer is 380 miles. (As an added bonus, we have discovered that the collision occurred at 8:00 PM, because $b = 6$. But the problem didn't ask for that information, so we keep it to ourselves.)

Following, are still further examples that benefit from a diagram.

EXAMPLES

○ *The area of a rectangle is 165 square feet. If both dimensions are decreased by 2 feet, the area will be 117. Find the dimensions of the original rectangle.*

SOLUTION:

This problem involves two rectangles, the original one and the one we have after we reduce both dimensions by 2 feet. We draw two diagrams side by side. We will label the dimensions of the first rectangle as x and y for the length and width respectively. (We won't use l and w, because those are the letters used in the $A = lw$ formula. We're going to be using that formula twice, once for each rectangle, so we don't want to be confused as to which of the two lengths l stands for.) In labeling the second rectangle, we will remember that its length is 2 less than the length of the first rectangle, and that its width is 2 less than the width of the first rectangle. Therefore the dimensions of the second rectangle are $x - 2$ for the length, and $y - 2$ for the width.

The advantage of the diagram in this case is not so much to provide information about the quantities as to clarify and reinforce the idea that we are talking about two <u>separate</u> rectangles:

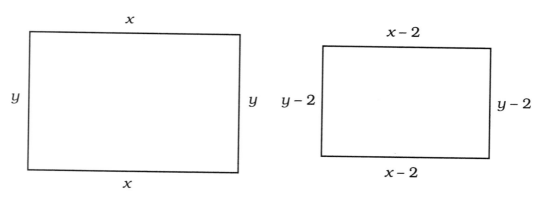

The other given information in the problem deals with the areas of the rectangles, so we use the $A = lw$ formula once for each rectangle in order to get our equations:

$$165 = xy$$
$$117 = (x - 2)(y - 2)$$

And the solutions are $x = 15$, $y = 11$, and $x = 11$, $y = 15$. As in an earlier example, on page 71, these are essentially the same solution. We choose to define the length as the larger number, 15, and the width as the smaller number, 11. We check the wording of the original problem and see that the requested information was the dimensions (i.e., the length and width) of the original rectangle. That's exactly what x and y were supposed to represent, and so 15 × 11 is the answer.

A rectangular garden is 40 feet by 30 feet. There is a sidewalk of uniform width bordering all four sides of the garden, and the total area of the sidewalk is 415.25 square feet. How wide is the sidewalk?

SOLUTION:

Without a diagram, this problem would probably be a challenge for almost anybody. But a diagram will make it manageable. The important point is to remember that the sidewalk has the same width at every point. So, there is only one unknown quantity (the width of the sidewalk), which we will creatively label as x.

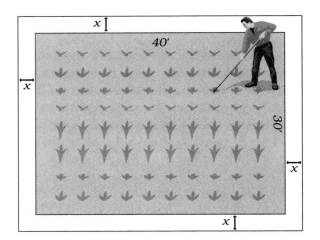

The diagram reveals several facts that might not be obvious if we were doing all the work in our heads. First of all, notice that the length of the entire plot of ground, *including the sidewalk*, is $40 + 2x$. Similarly, the width of the entire plot of ground is $30 + 2x$.

Armed with our observations, we could calculate the area of the entire sidewalk in terms of x, and then set that expression equal to 415.25. However, that would mean breaking the sidewalk up into separate pieces, and we would have to be careful to account for everything without allowing the pieces to overlap. However, the diagram gives us a simpler way to handle the problem. We can see that the area of the entire plot of ground is equal to the area of the garden plus the area of the sidewalk. And the area of the entire plot of ground is easier to express algebraically than the area of the sidewalk, because the entire plot of ground is one simple rectangle. Therefore, we set up the following quantities:

Area of the entire plot = $(40 + 2x)(30 + 2x)$
Area of the garden = $40 \times 30 = 1,200$
Area of the sidewalk = 415.25 (given)

We now have two ways of calculating the area of the entire plot: by multiplying $40 + 2x$ by $30 + 2x$, or by adding 1,200 and 415.25. Therefore, these two quantities must be equal, and we have our equation:

$(40 + 2x)(30 + 2x) = 1,200 + 415.25$
or
$4x^2 + 140x + 1,200 = 1,615.25$

The solution is 2.75 (–37.75 is also a solution, but we will of course ignore negative solutions). We had x represent the width of the sidewalk, which is the quantity the problem asked for, and so we are finished. The sidewalk is 2.75 feet, or 2 feet 9 inches, wide.

○ *A plane flew 100 miles northward, then turned due east, and flew 130 miles. How far was the plane from its starting point?*

SOLUTION:

If this problem is at all difficult for you, draw a diagram. It will immediately become easy:

The diagram shows clearly that the distance between the plane's starting point and ending point is the hypotenuse of a right triangle. The problem is a straightforward application of the Pythagorean Theorem, $a^2 + b^2 = c^2$. In this case, the "c" is unknown, and the "a" and "b" are the distance north, 100, and the distance east, 130. So the equation is:

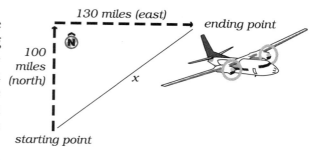

$$100^2 + 130^2 = x^2$$

and the solution is $x=\sqrt{26,900}$, or approximately 164 miles.

Exercise

1. The hypotenuse of a right triangle is 6 inches longer than one of the legs. The area is 38.4 square inches. How long is the other leg?

2. The area of a rectangle is $201\frac{1}{4}$ square miles. The perimeter is 58 miles. What are the dimensions?

3. What is the area of an 18-inch wide path surrounding a circle 35 feet in diameter?

4. There are three tables, each with a perimeter of 7 feet. The first table is circular, the second is a square, and the third is an isosceles right triangle. What is the total area of the three tables?

5. The radius of Circle #2 is 5 feet more than twice the radius of Circle #1. The total area of the two circles is 113.883 square feet. What is the radius of Circle #1?

6. Bingtown is 40 miles directly north of Bongtown. Bangtown is 75 miles directly west of Bingtown. How far is it from Bangtown to Bongtown?

7. Becky ran one circuit around a square track 1 mile on each side. She cut her speed in half each time she turned a corner. It took her 1.5 hours to make the complete circuit. How long did it take her to run the first mile?

TRIGONOMETRY PROBLEMS

Most word problems in trigonometry involve one or more triangles. There are six facts to know about any triangle: the lengths of the three sides, and the measures of the three angles. If we can find all six values for a triangle, then we say that we have "solved the triangle."

Since most story problems in trigonometry involve triangles, it is almost always helpful to draw a diagram.

Once you have drawn a diagram of the situation, you should decide if you are dealing with a right triangle. Problems with right triangles are solved differently from problems with other triangles. In general, if your triangle doesn't have a right angle, you will use the Law of Sines or the Law of Cosines to solve it. If the triangle does have a right angle, then you will just use the basic trigonometric functions—sine, cosine, and/or tangent—to solve the problem.

EXAMPLE

A flagpole makes a shadow 42 feet long. The angle of inclination from the horizontal to the sun is 37°. How tall is the flagpole?

SOLUTION:

This is a standard word problem in trigonometry. The important points to know are:

1. The pole makes a 90° angle with the ground.

2. The end of the shadow, the tip of the flagpole, and the sun are all on one straight line.

Armed with this information, we can draw a diagram:

The diagram shows that we have a right triangle. The value we want is the height (or length) of the flagpole. For the sake of completeness, it is often a good idea to write down all six values which describe the triangle, and identify which of them are unknown. Furthermore, it is a very good idea to identify one of the angles as the angle whose trigonometric functions you are going to work with, and designate each of the three

C

B

$\beta = 37°$

γ

$A = 42'$

sides as opposite, adjacent, or hypotenuse. **PLEASE NOTE THAT THIS COMMENT APPLIES ONLY TO RIGHT TRIANGLES!!** In this case, we'll use the trigonometric functions of the 37° angle. (It would be just as easy to use the functions of the other acute angle, which is 53°, but we have to choose one and stick with it.)

Sides:
    A = 42 (adjacent to the 37° angle)
    B = unknown (opposite to the 37° angle)
    C = unknown (hypotenuse)

Angles:
    α = 53° (90° – 37°)
    β = 37°
    γ = 90°

The value we are asked for is side B. If the unknown is the length of a side, the procedure will always be to use a length we *do* know along with the unknown, in an equation which defines one of the trigonometric functions. [It's probably useful to point out that if we don't know the length of at least one side, then we have no hope of solving the problem. That's because there are infinitely many triangles which have the angles 53°, 37°, and 90°. The sides could be a few millimeters each, or they could be millions of light-years each.]

The length we know is A = adjacent = 42. The length we want is B = opposite. Which of the primary trigonometric functions uses the adjacent side and the opposite side? The answer is the *tangent*. So we set up the equation which defines the tangent function:

$$\tan 37° = \frac{\text{opp}}{\text{adj}} = \frac{B}{42}$$

A calculator tells us that $\tan 37°$ = .753554, and we solve the equation to get B = 31.65 feet. If we want to convert to feet and inches, it's about 31 feet, 8 inches. Since B represents the height of the flagpole, and that height was what the problem asked for, we are finished. The answer is 31 feet, 8 inches.

Exercise

Paul Bearer was standing on the edge of a river and looking directly across at a tree on the opposite bank. He then walked 150 feet along the river bank and looked back across the river at the tree. His line of sight made an angle of 56.89° with the river bank. How wide is the river?

As we'll see in the example below, problems can be complicated by the need for some other formulas or calculations in addition to just the straightforward use of trigonometric functions.

EXAMPLE

The pilot of a law enforcement plane knows that a drug-smuggling plane is exactly two hundred miles west of her plane and heading due north at 350 mph. Her plane can fly 650 mph. At what angle with respect to due north should she fly in order to intercept the other plane, and how long will it take her to catch it?

SOLUTION:

In this problem, there is definitely a triangle, but only one length and one angle are given:

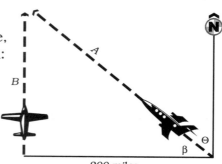

200 miles

(Note that the angle θ is needed in the diagram, because we were asked for the angle the pilot should make with respect to *due north*. That angle is not part of the triangle, but we can get it easily once we know the measures of the angles in the triangle. We know about the 90° angle because north and west make a right angle with each other.)

Without some further information, it requires *three* of the six values in a triangle to be known before we can solve it. The information we have not yet used is that the drug smuggler's plane goes 350 mph, and the law enforcement plane goes 650 mph. For the moment, that converts the problem into a rate-time-distance problem, and there are two trips: the smuggler's and the law enforcement officer's. As always, the formula which governs the action is $rt = d$ for both trips. We are given r in both cases, and we note that *the time will be the same for both trips*, since the law enforcement plane intends to intercept the drug-smuggling plane. Therefore we will need only one t:

Law enforcement plane:

  $r = 650$
  $t = t$ (unknown)
  $d = A$ (side A above)

Drug smuggler's plane:

  $r = 350$
  $t = t$
  $d = B$ (side B above)

Now, the two occurrences of the formula $rt = d$ give us:

  $650t = A$
  $350t = B$

and so we can fill in our diagram with $650t$ for A, and $350t$ for B.

Looking at the diagram, we now see that we can express all three sides using only one unknown. Since this is a <u>right</u> triangle, that means we can use the Pythagorean Theorem to solve for that one unknown (t):

$$(350t)^2 + 200^2 = (650t)^2$$

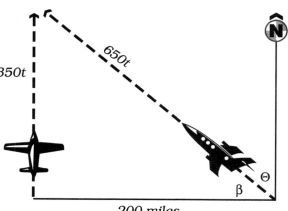

The solution to the equation is t = 0.365, which is expressed in hours since the rates were expressed in miles per hour. Looking back at the original problem, we see that we have found one of the two answers we needed; namely, the time it will take the pilot to catch the plane. That time is .365 × 60 = 21.9 minutes. To find the heading the pilot should use, we note that angle $\theta + \beta = 90°$, so we'll get the answer easily if we find β.

200 miles

Now that we have a value for t, we can easily find the lengths of the two unknown sides and then use that information to get β. The hypotenuse of the triangle is $650t = 650(.365) = 237.25$. We already know that the side adjacent to β is 200. The trigonometric function which uses the hypotenuse and the adjacent is the cosine. Set up the equation:

$$\cos \beta = \frac{200}{237.25}$$

or

$$\beta = \cos^{-1}\left(\frac{200}{237.25}\right) = 32.58°$$

As we noted above, the angle we were asked for is θ, and so we solve for $\theta + \beta = 90°$, and get

$$\theta = 90° - 32.58° = 57.42°$$

It will take 21.9 minutes to catch the plane if she heads at 57.42° west of due north.

Exercise

A pilot flying at 32,000 feet altitude and 340 mph looks down at a searchlight on the ground. The angle of depression of his line of sight to the searchlight is 35.49°. If he keeps on flying in the direction he is going, he will go directly over the searchlight. How long will it take him to get there?

One commonly seen type of trigonometry word problem involves two right triangles, and seems unsolvable at first glance. But it isn't!

EXAMPLE

○ *Delores Mae Shepard is driving toward a mountain at 60 mph. The angle of elevation of her line of sight to the top of the mountain is 2.39°. One hour later, the angle of elevation to the top of the same mountain is 25°. How high is the mountain?*

SOLUTION:

The author of this book confesses that when he first saw this problem, he thought there wasn't enough information to solve it. "Don't we need to know the distance from the car to the mountain, in at least *one* of those two points in time?" I asked (and I was a math teacher at the time!). The answer is no, we don't. Let's draw a diagram:

(The 60-mile distance comes from the fact that Helen drove that distance in one hour, going at 60 mph.)

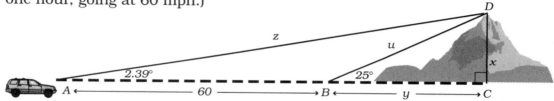

What we see here is that there are two right triangles, ACD and BCD. It is true that we don't have enough information to solve either of them directly, but we will see that we can solve the two of them simultaneously! That's because if we look at the equations which define the tangent of 2.39° and the tangent of 25°, there will be only two unknowns. Here are the definitions of the quantities for the two triangles:

    Triangle ACD:
        $60 + y$ = side adjacent to 2.39°
        x = side opposite to 2.39°
        z = hypotenuse (we won't use z at all, but we include it for
            completeness)

    Triangle BCD:
        y = side adjacent to 25°
        x = side opposite to 25°
        u = hypotenuse (which, again, we won't use)

The equations which define the tangents of 2.39° and 25° are:

$$\tan 2.39° = \frac{x}{60+y}$$

$$\tan 25° = \frac{x}{y}$$

Solving those two equations simultaneously (perhaps the easiest method is to substitute $x = y \tan 25°$ into the first equation), the answer is $x = 2.75$,

83

$y = 5.898$. We remember that our distances have been expressed in *miles* throughout the problem, so we convert to feet for the height of the mountain (x):

$$2.75\left(\tfrac{5280 \text{ feet}}{1 \text{ mile}}\right) = 14{,}520 \text{ feet}$$

Finally, we look at an example in which the triangle involved is not a right triangle.

EXAMPLE

A triangular race requires the runners to run a straight leg of 80 yards, then make a turn and run a second straight leg of 100 yards, make a second turn and run a final straight leg of 115 yards, which brings them back to the starting point. Through how many degrees will the runners turn on the first turn?

SOLUTION:

The information is straightforward, allowing us to draw a diagram immediately, although we make note of the fact that the angle through which the runners turn will be outside the triangle. We can see that we do not have a right triangle here (or if we do, that information isn't given). What we have is a triangle in which all three sides are given, but no angles. That is a Law of Cosines situation. We want to set it up so that the angle α is in the equation, which means we have this:

$$115^2 = 80^2 + 100^2 - 2(80)(100)\cos\alpha$$

The solution to this equation is $\cos\alpha = 0.1984375$, which gives $\alpha = 78.55°$. Then we solve $\alpha + \theta = 180°$, and get $\theta = 101.45°$. Since θ is the angle through which the runners turn, we have our solution.

Exercise

1. A woman looks up at the roof of a skyscraper while standing on the other side of a 45-foot-wide street. The angle of elevation of her line of sight is 85.32°. How tall is the building?

2. Yubindrinkin Avenue and Line Drive merge at an angle of 75°. How far apart (in a straight line) are Jerry Atrick, who is walking 65 yards from the intersection on Yubindrinkin Avenue, and Dinah Sawyer, who is walking on Line Drive, 85 yards from the intersection?

3. The minute hand of a clock is 4 inches long. At 5:00, the straight-line distance between the tips of the hands is 5.352 inches. How long is the hour hand?

4. A 35-foot flagpole casts a 44-foot shadow. What is the angle of elevation of the sun?

5. How long is a ladder which makes a 70° angle with the ground and leans against a spot on the wall 10 feet above the ground?

6. Assuming that the radius of the earth is 4000 miles, what is the distance around the earth at a latitude of 35° north of the equator? (Hints: The 35° latitude line forms a circle. The radius of that circle is a leg of a right triangle whose hypotenuse is a radius of the earth. The other leg is a piece of the earth's axis perpendicular to the plane of the 35° latitude. The 35° latitude gets its name from the fact that the radius of the earth drawn out to the 35° latitude makes a 35° angle with a radius drawn to the equator. Draw a diagram!)

7. In a football game, a runner is on the 40-yard line, 10 yards from the left sideline, and heading for the goal line. He is trying to outrun a defender at the 35-yard line who is 20 yards from the left sideline. Both players are heading for the intersection between the goal line and the left sideline, and they are running at the same speed. Will the runner score a touchdown or will he be tackled before he gets there?

8. In problem 7 above, what is the angle between the route of the runner and the route of the defender?

9. A helicopter is rising straight upward. At one point a passenger in the helicopter sees a pond on the ground, and the angle of depression of his line of sight is 21.8°. The helicopter rises an additional 1,200 feet, and the angle of depression when he looks at the pond is now 45°. How far is the pond from the point where the helicopter took off?

10. Willy Makeit can run 12 mph and can swim 2 mph. He looks across a river which is 320 feet wide. On the opposite bank, and downriver from where he is standing, he sees a scalper selling tickets to a Garth Brooks concert. His line of sight makes an angle of 18° with the river. How long will it take Willy to run down to the point directly opposite the scalper, and then swim across the river?

CALCULUS PROBLEMS

In this section, we will deal with three types of word problems commonly found in differential calculus courses: optimization, velocity and acceleration, and related rates problems. An understanding of this material requires that the reader be familiar with the methods of differentiation (including implicit differentiation) and with maximizing and minimizing of functions.

Optimization Problems

An optimization problem asks us to find out how to get the largest or smallest possible value for some quantity. The first and most important step in solving optimization problems is the same as the first and most important step in solving algebra word problems: DEFINE YOUR QUANTITIES!!

However, the "define your quantities" step has an additional requirement in optimization problems. We must identify which variable quantity is the quantity to be maximized or minimized. In the following paragraphs, we will refer to the quantity to be maximized or minimized as Q.

Once we have identified Q, we need to express Q as a function of one other quantity in the problem. This step often has to be broken down into two steps: First, express Q as a function of any number of variables in the problem. In most cases, this step should be comparatively simple. Second, use the information given in the problem about relationships among the quantities to reduce the number of variables in the function so that we have $Q =$ a function of only one variable. That second step is likely to be the most complicated part of the problem.

After finding the function, we use standard calculus procedures to maximize or minimize the function, <u>subject to the domain</u>. The domain is sometimes given, or sometimes it is established by common sense (for example, in many story problems, negative values for some of the variables will make no sense).

Once we have maximized or minimized the function, we **look back at the original problem** to see which values we were asked for. This is a more important issue in optimization problems than in most algebra problems because there are usually two reasonable possibilities for the requested answer. We might be asked for the highest or lowest possible value for Q, or we might be asked what value of some other variable will give us that maximum or minimum value of Q. After maximizing or minimizing the function, we shouldn't have too much trouble finding the value the problem asks for, <u>as long as we pay attention to what it DID ask us for</u>!

Ben Dover wants to use 480 yards of fencing to create a fenced, rectangular area in his pasture. The fenced area will be divided into 6 smaller areas as shown in the diagram. What should be the dimensions of the entire fenced rectangle so that the total area of the fenced portion is as large as possible?

SOLUTION:

The people who gave us this problem were nice enough to give us a diagram for free, so we simply use the diagram to label the quantities we will be dealing with. Before we do so, however, notice that the placement of the fences which divide the larger area into smaller areas will have nothing to do with the problem. The two fences which run vertically inside the rectangle will always be the same length as the width of the rectangle, and the fence which runs horizontally inside the rectangle will always be the same length as the length of the rectangle. The only real variable quantities are the length, the width, and the area of the (larger) rectangle. (The area of the rectangle is not an explicit dimension of the diagram. But we know it is going to be one of our quantities, because it's the quantity the problem asked us to maximize.)

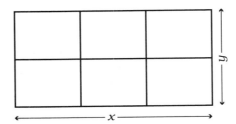

Now we list the significant quantities in the problem:

A = area of the large rectangle
x = length of the large rectangle
y = width of the large rectangle

We have already identified A as the quantity to be maximized. So we want to express A as a function of other quantities in the problem. This is easy, of course, because the area of a rectangle is equal to the length times the width. Therefore our function is:

$A = xy$

The function above (xy) is *not* the function we want to maximize or minimize, because it has two variables. However, the function we will maximize or minimize *will* be a "direct descendant" of xy. What we must do is to change the xy to some expression involving only one variable.

The information we haven't used yet is the total amount of fencing (480 yards). If we can use that fact to build an equation involving x and y, we will solve that equation for one of the variables and make a substitution in $A = xy$.

A look at the diagram shows that the total amount of fencing amounts to 4 widths of the rectangle (in other words, $4y$), and 3 lengths (which is $3x$). Therefore we have this equation:

$$3x + 4y = 480$$

This equation is easy to solve for y, and we get:

$$y = \frac{480 - 3x}{4} = 120 - \frac{3}{4}x$$

We now use that equation to substitute for y in the formula $A = xy$, and we will have the one-variable function we are looking for:

$$A = x(120 - \frac{3}{4}x) = 120x - \frac{3}{4}x^2$$

Now we have a function which we can maximize. We do NOT do that by immediately differentiating and setting the derivative equal to zero. We <u>first</u> decide what the domain of the function is. Remembering that x stands for the length of the rectangle, we ask ourselves what are the reasonable values for the length. First, we notice that the length must of course be positive. Second, we realize that there are three fences of length x in the arrangement, and that all the fences put together add up to 480. Therefore, the largest possible x is $\frac{480}{3} = 160$. Our domain for this function is $0 \le x \le 160$.

Now we maximize the function $120x - \frac{3}{4}x^2$, subject to the domain $0 \le x \le 160$, using standard calculus procedures, and find that the maximum occurs when $x = 80$.

The original problem asked us for the *dimensions* of the rectangle which give us the greatest possible area. Looking at the diagram, we see that the dimensions are x and y. We have already found the value of x; it's 80 yards. We have a nice formula we can use to find y now that we have x. This is an example of why it helps to keep track of your work! We found earlier that

$$y = 120 - \frac{3}{4}x$$

and therefore, the value of y which corresponds to $x = 80$ is $120 - \frac{3}{4}(80) = 60$.

The dimensions which give the largest area are 80 × 60 yards.

Ben Dover wants to use 480 yards of fencing to create a fenced, rectangular area in his pasture. The fenced area will be divided into 6 smaller areas as shown in the previous diagram. What is the largest possible area for the rectangular area?

SOLUTION:

This problem is not identical to the previous one. In this problem, we are asked for the *largest possible area* instead of the dimensions which will *give* the largest area. The problem would be done exactly the same way as the previous one, until we get to the point where we write an answer in the answer blank on the test! At that point, we realize that our value for x is <u>not</u> what the problem asked for; x stands for the length of the rectangle, NOT the area. However, we *do* have a function which will give us the area as soon as we know the length:

$$A = 120x - \frac{3}{4}x^2$$

Substituting $x = 80$ into the function, we get $A = 4,800$. So the largest possible area is 4,800 square yards.

Exercise

A piece of wire 21.4248 inches long is to be cut into two pieces. One piece will be bent into a circle, and the other piece will be bent into a square. How big should each piece be in order to maximize the total area of the two shapes?

EXAMPLE

An Internet service provider finds that 5000 people will subscribe to the service if the charge is $35 per month. They estimate that for each $1 reduction in the monthly fee, an additional 600 more people will sign up. What price should they charge in order to get the maximum revenue?

We looked at a *similar* problem in Chapters 2 and 3 on Defining Quantities and Reducing the Number of Variables. In that problem, however, we were asked to find what price should be charged to get exactly $257,600 in revenue. This time, we are asked how to get the **maximum** revenue — which might well be more than $257,600.

[Quick common sense exercise: Theoretically, the maximum possible revenue might be *less* than $257,600. But if so, then the original problem (finding the price which would yield exactly $257,600 in revenue) must have been impossible. Why?]

When we defined the variables in Chapter 3, on pages 47-48, we started with the following setup (go back and review that discussion if you need to):

> S = number of subscribers
> F = monthly fee
> D = number of $1 reductions from the original $35 fee

Of course, in that problem we knew exactly what the total revenue was going to be: $257,600. In this case, the revenue is a variable quantity. So we want to define total revenue as a variable also. If we use R, that will give us:

> S = number of subscribers
> F = monthly fee
> D = number of $1 reductions from the original $35 fee
> R = total revenue

Moreover, the total revenue is the quantity we want to maximize. So we now express R as a function of other variables. It isn't too hard to realize that we get the revenue by multiplying the monthly fee by the number of subscribers. So our preliminary function is:

> $R = FS$

Now we want to reduce the function to use just one variable. In Chapter 3, on page 48, we discovered that we could express both F and S in terms of D:

> D = number of reductions from the original $35 fee
> $5000 + 600D$ = number of subscribers = S
> $35 - D$ = fee = F

So we can substitute $5,000 + 600D$ for S, and $35 - D$ for F, and we'll have:

> $R = (35 - D) (5,000 + 600D)$

Now we look at the domain of this function. In this case, negative values are probably OK for D, because it's just possible that we would get the maximum amount of revenue by *raising* the fee (which would mean a negative number of "decreases"). On the other hand, since we would lose 600 subscribers for each $1 increase (that would be a "gain" of "negative 600" people), we couldn't possibly raise the fee by more than $9.00, because $9 \times 600 = 5,400$, which is more subscribers than we have to begin with. So the smallest possible value of D can't be equal to or less than –9. At the other end of the scale, we obviously can't reduce the fee by more than $35, because we would be charging a negative fee in that case—which is very unlikely to maximize our revenue! So we will use the domain of $-9 < D \le 35$.

Maximizing the function $R = (35 - D) (5,000 + 600D)$ subject to the domain, we find that the maximum occurs where $D = 13\frac{1}{3}$. Now, if we assume that the fee reductions will be whole multiples of $1, we must check to see whether a $13 or a $14 reduction would give us a greater amount of revenue. No, we <u>can't</u> just assume that since 13 is closer to $13\frac{1}{3}$ than 14 is, that 13 would be the right answer. We must try both numbers on either side of $13\frac{1}{3}$. If we substitute $D = 13$, we will find that $R = (35 - 13) (5,000 + 600 \times 13) = 281,600$. If we substitute $D = 14$, we get $R = 281,400$. Therefore the whole-dollar amount of reduction should be $13.

Now we look again at the original problem to see exactly what we were asked for. The value we need is the price to be charged, in other words, the monthly fee. D does not stand for the fee, and neither does R. Looking back at the definitions of our quantities, we see that the monthly fee, F, is $35 - D$, which is $35 - 13 = 22$. Therefore a fee of $22 (to the nearest dollar) will maximize revenue.

In some optimization problems, we can maximize or minimize the requested quantity by maximizing or minimizing some other related quantity. Two instances are:

1. A distance is maximized or minimized if the *square* of the distance is maximized or minimized. This idea comes in handy when the distance is calculated using the distance formula $d = \sqrt{(x_1 - x_2)^2 - (y_1 + y_2)^2}$, or when the distance is one leg of a right triangle and we use the Pythagorean Theorem to calculate the distance.

2. An **acute** angle can be maximized or minimized if the *tangent* of the angle is maximized. This works because for angles between 0° and 90°, the tangent gets bigger as the angle gets bigger.

EXAMPLE

Hugh R. Yew is in an art museum, looking at a mural 3 feet high. The bottom of the mural is one foot higher than his eye level. How far away should Hugh stand so that the angle of view filled by the mural is maximized?

SOLUTION:

Here is a diagram of the situation.

The quantity to be maximized in the problem is angle α. We want to know the value of the variable which will maximize α. We can accomplish this

92

by maximizing the *tangent* of α, because clearly α will be less than 90°. It is true that α is not part of a right triangle, so we don't immediately know what the tangent of α is. But we notice that α can be thought of as the sum of angles α and β, minus angle β. Since the sum of α and β is part of a right triangle (HAC), and β is also part of a right triangle (HAB), we can express the tangents of those angles in terms of x. Then we can use the formula for the tangent of the difference between two angles to express the tangent of α.

Let's set up the quantities for the two right triangles HAB and HAC:

Triangle HAB:
  x = side adjacent to β
  1= side opposite to β
  y = hypotenuse (which we won't need)

Triangle HAC:
  x = side adjacent to $\alpha + \beta$
  4 = side opposite to $\alpha + \beta$
  z = hypotenuse (which we also won't need)

From the quantities above, we set up the tangents of β and of $\alpha + \beta$:

$$\tan \beta = \tfrac{1}{x}$$
$$\tan(\alpha + \beta) = \tfrac{4}{x}$$

Then we use the formula for the tangent of the difference between two angles:

$$\tan(u - v) = \frac{\tan u - \tan \beta}{1 + \tan u \tan v}$$

In our case, this translates into:

$$\tan \alpha = \tan\big[(\alpha + \beta) - \beta\big] = \frac{\tan(\alpha + \beta) - \tan \beta}{1 + \tan(\alpha + \beta)\tan \beta}$$

$$= \frac{\tfrac{4}{x} - \tfrac{1}{x}}{1 + \left(\tfrac{4}{x}\right)\left(\tfrac{1}{x}\right)} = \frac{3x}{x^2 + 4}$$

(Yes it is; work it out for yourself!)

Now we maximize the function $\frac{3x}{x^2 + 4}$. The domain will be all positive numbers, since for all we know Hugh might have to stand 9 million miles away. The maximum will occur when $x = 2$. Since x stands for the quantity we were asked about (the distance from the mural at which Hugh should stand in order to get the widest view), the answer is 2 feet, and we are finished.

Exercise

Find the point (x- and y-coordinates) on the line y = 2x – 3 which is closest to the point (9,4). [Hint: Minimize the square of the distance between (9,4) and any point on the line.]

Velocity-Acceleration Problems

Velocity- acceleration problems in calculus are generally different from the rate- time-distance problems in algebra because **the velocity is not constant**. If the velocity (rate) is not constant, then the formula *rt = d* simply does not apply. Instead, the position of the moving object, the velocity of the object, and the acceleration of the object are all *functions of time*. Furthermore:

    1. The velocity function is the derivative of the position function.
    2. The acceleration function is the derivative of the velocity function, and therefore the *second* derivative of the position function.

In particular, if the gravity of the earth is the only force acting on a rising or falling object, then the acceleration is a constant –32 feet per second squared (the negative sign refers to the convention that we regard the positive direction as "up"). This leads to the following formulas:

$$v = v_0 - 32t$$
$$h = h_0 + v_0 t - 16t^2$$

where:

    v = the velocity at time t
    h = the height at time t
    v_0 = the velocity
    h_0 = the height
    t = the number of *seconds* since the time of the height and velocity

EXAMPLE

Phyllis Ophical drops a stone from a bridge. The stone hits the water 3.873 seconds later. How high is the bridge?

SOLUTION:

Using the variables as defined in the formulas above, the unknown in this problem is h_0, the initial height. When the problem says that the stone hit the water after 3.873 seconds, we are being told that $h = 0$ when $t = 3.873$. Furthermore, when the problem states that the stone was "dropped" (as opposed to *thrown*), we know that the initial velocity was *zero* —Phyllis didn't put any additional velocity into it. So we have the following values for our quantities:

h_0 = initial height (unknown)
h = height at time $t = 0$
t = time = 3.873
v_0 = initial velocity = 0
v = velocity at time t (unknown)

Looking at the formulas given earlier, we can see that the formula

$$h = h_0 + v_0 t - 16t^2$$

is the formula we want to use. We know that because the unknown h_0 is part of the formula, and because we have values for all the other variables in the formula. Therefore we should be able to form an equation which we can solve with no further complications. Making the appropriate substitutions, we have:

$$0 = h_0 + (0)(3.873) - 16(3.873)^2$$

and the solution is h_0 = 240 feet. Since h_0 is the quantity we were asked for, we are finished.

Exercise

Luke Warm threw a stone down from the same bridge, and the stone hit the water in exactly three seconds. With what initial velocity did Luke throw the stone?

Related Rates

A "related rates" problem is a word problem in which two quantities, which we will call Q_1 and Q_2, have some permanent mathematical relationship, and Q_1 is changing at some given rate. The problem asks us to find the rate at which Q_2 is changing. As usual, the first critical step is to identify the quantities. This step should include identifying Q_1 and Q_2.

After we have identified the important quantities, we need to establish the mathematical relationship between Q_1 and Q_2. This does not require that we express Q_2 as a function of Q_1, or vice versa. It simply means that we build an equation which includes both Q_1 and Q_2, *and which remains true throughout the motion or changes in quantities.* The reason for this last requirement is that we want to find the rate at which quantities are changing—and we know from the theory of calculus that we cannot accomplish this by looking at just one point in time.

Once we have built the equation described in the previous paragraph, we differentiate the equation implicitly with respect to time, remembering that both Q_1 and Q_2 are functions of time. Our equation should now include both $\frac{dQ_1}{dt}$ and $\frac{dQ_2}{dt}$.

Since we are asked for the rate at which Q_2 is changing, $\frac{dQ_2}{dt}$ is our unknown. We can usually solve the differentiated equation for $\frac{dQ_2}{dt}$ easily, since we are usually given the value of $\frac{dQ_1}{dt}$. There are sometimes other variables for which we need to substitute values in order to solve for $\frac{dQ_2}{dt}$, but those values are usually provided in the problem as well.

EXAMPLE

A jet is flying 8 miles high at 720 mph. A searchlight, positioned directly under the path of the jet, is trained on the jet. How fast is the angle of elevation of the searchlight's beam changing when the jet passes directly overhead?

SOLUTION:

A diagram of the situation is shown here.

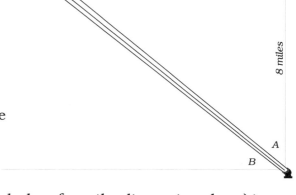

The angle of elevation is angle B, but we will set up our equation using angle A instead. We choose to do that because angle A is part of a triangle which includes the jet's path, and because angle A is decreasing at exactly the same rate as angle B is increasing (Right? Think about it!).

The quantity whose rate of change is given (Q_1, to use our vocabulary from the discussion above) is x. The quantity whose rate of change we *want* (Q_2) is angle A. The significant quantities are:

> x = distance from the jet to the position directly over the searchlight
>   (quantity whose rate of change is given)
> A = angle through which the searchlight is moving
>   (quantity whose rate of change we want)
> 8 = height of the jet, and the side adjacent to angle A in the right
>   triangle

We want an equation which includes both x and A, and which remains true throughout the motion of the jet. It is not hard to see that the equation we want is:

$$\tan A = \tfrac{x}{8}$$

Remembering that both A and x are functions of time (t), we differentiate the equation implicitly with respect to t, and get:

$$\sec^2 A \, \frac{dA}{dt} = \tfrac{1}{8} \frac{dx}{dt}$$

Since the jet is moving at 720 mph, we know that $\frac{dx}{dt} = -720$. The negative is because the jet is coming *closer* to the searchlight, thereby decreasing the value of x. Furthermore, now (*and only now*), we can use the fact that the particular point in time we want is when the jet is directly overhead. At that moment, angle A is zero, and the secant of 0 is 1. Therefore, our equation is:

$$\left(1^2\right)\frac{dA}{dt} = \frac{1}{8}(-720)$$
$$= -90$$

This means that angle A is decreasing at a rate of 90 *radians per hour*. "*Radians*" because derivatives of trigonometric functions only work with radians, and "per hour" because the speed of the jet was expressed in miles per hour. Since A is *decreasing* at 90 radians per hour, angle B is *increasing* at 90 radians per hour.

Exercise

Convert the "radians per hour" answer in the previous problem into degrees per second.

Exercise

A 15-foot ladder is leaning against a wall. The foot of the ladder is being pulled out at 8 inches per second. How fast is the top of the ladder falling when it (the top of the ladder) is exactly 12 feet high?

Exercise

1. Find two positive numbers with a product of 288, and with a sum as small as possible.

2. A health club offers memberships for $300 per year if 100 or fewer people join. If more than 100 people join, the club will reduce the membership fee by $1 per person (for everybody) for each additional member over 100. How many members would maximize the total revenue for the club?

3. Find the point on the parabola $y = x^2$ which is closest to the point (5,4). (You may need approximation methods to solve the resulting equation.)

4. We have a rectangular piece of cardboard, 12 feet by 5 feet. We are going to form an open box (i.e., with no lid) by cutting out squares of equal size from the four corners and then bending the cardboard up to form sides of the box. How big should the squares be in order to get the largest possible box (in volume)?

5. We want to construct the lower base and two sides of a trapezoid in such a way that (1) the base and the two sides are each 1 foot long, (2) the angles between the lower base and the two sides are equal, and (3) the area of the trapezoid is as great as possible. What should the angles at the bottom of the trapezoid be in order to accomplish this?

6. If a particle is traveling along the parabola $y = 2x^2 - 5x + 3$, and passes through the point $(4, 15)$ at a rate such that the y-coordinate is increasing at 2 units per second, then how fast is the x-coordinate changing at that point?

7. A vertical cross-section along the length of a swimming pool is a trapezoid whose bases are 50 feet at the top and 40 feet at the bottom, and whose height is 12 feet. The surface of the pool is a (so that the volume is the product of 25 and the area of the trapezoid). If the pool is being filled at the rate of 1.2 cubic feet per minute, how fast is the water level rising at the point when there are 6,375 cubic feet of water in the pool?

8. A searchlight aboard a ship 6 miles from shore is revolving at the rate of one revolution every 18 seconds. How fast is the beam moving along the (straight) shoreline at a point when the beam makes a 60° angle with the shoreline?

9. The diameter of a sphere is increasing at the rate of 2 feet per minute. How fast is the volume increasing at the point where the volume is 420 cubic feet?

10. Two cars are on a collision course toward point P. The paths of the two cars make a 30° angle with each other. The first car is 40 miles from P, and traveling toward P at 16 mph. The second car is 50 miles from P, and traveling at 20 mph. How fast is the (direct line) distance between the two cars decreasing? (Hint: Use the Law of Cosines.)

EXERCISES

This section includes exercises which do not require a knowledge of trigonometry or calculus. Trigonometry and calculus exercises are given at the ends of Chapters 7 and 8.

In the first 12 exercises, define the variable(s) and then write the requested quantity as a simplified algebraic expression involving the variable(s). Beginning with exercise 13, solve the entire problem.

1. A number minus the difference between the number and two.

2. The sum of one-third of a number and two-fifths of the number.

3. Three times the product of eleven and a number.

4. The difference between the product of twelve and a number, and one more than the number.

5. The difference between the square of a number and the total of twelve and six times the number.

6. The sum of twelve times a number and five added to the product of sixteen and the number.

7. Given that the sum of two numbers is twenty-one: The sum of twice the smaller number and two more than the larger number.

8. Given that the sum of two numbers is 43: The difference between seven more than the smaller number and twice the larger number.

9. The planet Pluto is about 26 times as far from the Earth (on average) as the planet Mars is. If x = the distance from the Earth to Mars, express the distance from the Earth to Pluto in terms of x.

10. In the 1988 presidential election, George Bush received 193,969 more votes than Michael Dukakis in the state of Mississippi. If x = the number of votes received by Michael Dukakis, express the number of votes for George Bush in terms of x.

11. Angle A is twice as big as angle B. Angle C is twice as big as angle A. If B = measure of angle B, express the measures of angles A and C in terms of B.

12. The total flying time on a round trip between New York and Los Angeles is 12 hours, but the time for the eastbound and westbound trips are not equal. If the time for the eastbound trip is t, express the time for the westbound trip in terms of t.

13. Find three consecutive integers with a sum of 243.

14. Find three consecutive even integers with a sum of -186.

15. Find three consecutive integers such that twice the smallest is 8 more than the largest.

16. Find three consecutive odd integers such that three times the largest is 51 more than twice the smallest.

17. Find four consecutive even integers with a sum of -332.

18. Find three consecutive integers such that the sum of the first, twice the second, and three times the third is 320.

19. Find two consecutive integers such that four times the larger integer is 188 less than six times the smaller.

20. The sum of the reciprocals of two consecutive integers is five times the reciprocal of their product. Find the integers.

21. The sum of the reciprocals of two consecutive even integers equals 14 times the product of their reciprocals. Find the integers.

22. Find two consecutive odd integers such that three times the first minus one-third the second equals $\frac{278}{3}$.

23. Find four consecutive integers such that the sum of the second integer and the fourth integer is 172.

24. The sum of the reciprocals of two consecutive even integers equals 22 times the product of their reciprocals. Find the integers.

25. What is the (simple) interest rate if $5,120 grows to $5,555.20 in 2 years?

26. What is the (simple) interest rate if $1,000 grows to $1,210 in 2 years?

27. What is the (simple) interest rate if $1,000 grows to $1,122.50 in 2 years?

28. The number d of diagonals of a polygon of n sides is:

$$d = \frac{n^2 - 3n}{2}$$

A polygon has 44 diagonals. How many sides does it have?

29. A ladder 13 feet long leans against a wall. The bottom of the ladder is 5 feet from the wall. How much farther would the bottom of the ladder have to be pulled away from the wall in order for the top of the ladder to drop by the same distance?

30. A baseball diamond is a square, 90 feet on a side. How far is it from home plate to second base?

31. Train A leaves San Itary heading due north. Train B leaves the same city at the same time, traveling west. Train A travels 14 mph faster than Train B. After 5 hours they are 130 miles apart. How fast is each train traveling?

32. An object is dropped from an airplane 2,048 feet above the ground. How long does it take to reach the ground?

33. An object is thrown down from an airplane 2,048 feet above the ground, with an initial velocity of 40 feet per second. How long does it take to reach the ground?

34. An object is thrown down from an airplane 2,048 feet above the ground, with an initial velocity of 40 feet per second. How far will it fall in the first 5 seconds?

35. The world record for a free fall to the earth by a woman without a parachute is 175 feet. How long did the fall take?

The next two problems will be much easier if you know the quadratic formula and how to solve two equations in two unknowns.

36. Percy Kewtion bought a group of lots for $913,000. The investor sold all but 3 of them for a total of $712,000. The selling price for each lot was $6,000 more than the original purchase price had been. How many lots were bought originally?

37. A sorority is going to spend $306 for a party. When 11 new pledges join the sorority, this reduces each student's cost by $1.65. How much did it cost each student before?

38. The sides of triangle A are 25 feet, 25 feet, and 30 feet. Triangle B is similar to A, and two of the sides of triangle B are 40 feet long each. How long is the third side?

39. If a number is decreased by 14 and the result is then divided by 5, the answer is 15. Find the number.

40. If three times a number is increased by 11 and the result is 47, what is the number?

41. One number is 18 more than a second number. If their sum is 62, find the numbers.

42. One number is 4 times a second number, and their sum is 65. Find the numbers.

43. One number is 7 more than another number. Three times the larger number exceeds four times the smaller number by 5. Find the numbers.

44. Five times the first of three consecutive even integers is 2 less than twice the sum of the second and third. Find the three integers.

45. The perimeter of an isosceles triangle is 39 inches. The third side is 15 inches shorter than either of the two equal sides. Find the lengths of the three sides.

46. The width of a rectangle is $\frac{2}{3}$ of its length. The perimeter is 140 feet. Find the dimensions.

47. Emma Nemm has $18,000. She invests part of her money at $7\frac{1}{2}\%$, and the rest at 9%. If her income for one year from the two investments was $1,560, then how much did she invest at each rate?

48. Grace made two investments, totaling $18,000. She made a 12% profit on one investment, but took a 15% loss on the other. Her net profit from the two investments was $945. How much was each investment?

49. Fouad has $10,000 invested at 6%. How much more must he invest at 12% to realize a net return of $9\frac{1}{2}\%$?

50. A trucking firm has two mixtures of antifreeze. One is 30% alcohol, and the other is 70% alcohol. How much of each must be mixed to get 80 gallons of a mixture which is 54% alcohol?

51. A company has 2500 gallons of an 11% pesticide solution. How much 4% pesticide solution should they add to that, in order to get a solution which is 8% pesticide?

52. A wire with a length given as x inches is bent into a square. Express the length of one side of the square in terms of x.

53. Wassamatta U. consists of three colleges: business, engineering, and fine arts. There are 2,900 students in the business college, 1,500 students in the engineering college, and 1,000 students in the fine arts college. What percent of the total student body is in the fine arts college?

54. A ski vacation package regularly costs $850 for one week, including lift tickets. By making an early reservation, a person receives a 15% discount. How much is the early reservation discount?

55. An airline deliberately sells 18% more tickets for a flight than the available number of seats (because they know that some people won't show up). The airline sold 177 seats for the flight. How many seats were actually available?

56. Two numbers are in a ratio of 3:5. The sum of the numbers is 104. Find the numbers.

57. I am 6 years younger than Ray Needay. The sum of our ages is 54. How old is each of us?

58. A woman is 6 years older than 5 times her house's age. The sum of the owner's age and the house's age is 48 years. How old is the house?

59. A purse contains twice as many nickels as dimes. The total value of the nickels and dimes is $2.40. How many nickels are in the purse?

60. A set of stamps consists of 23¢ stamps and 32¢ stamps. There are a total of 8 stamps, and the total value of the stamps is $1.93. How many of each type of stamp are there?

61. One side of a triangle is half the length of the longest side. The third side is 9 inches less than the longest side. The perimeter of the triangle is 186 inches. How long is each side?

62. I am two years younger than my sister. In 7 years, the sum of our ages will be 110. How old am I?

63. A motorboat traveled upstream in 6 hours, and then returned to its starting position in 3 hours. The speed of the boat in still water is 7 mph. How fast is the current?

64. A motorboat traveled downstream in 5 hours, and returned upstream in 7 hours. The current is 3 mph. What is the speed of the boat in still water?

65. A jet plane traveled with the wind for 240 miles, then turned around and flew against the wind for 192 miles. The two parts of the trip took an equal amount of time. The speed of the jet in still air is 360 mph. How long did the total trip take?

66. A 65-foot piece of rope is cut into 3 pieces, with each piece being three times as long as the previous one. What is the length of the longest piece?

67. A 178-foot cable is to be cut into four pieces, with each piece being 3 feet longer than the previous one. Find the lengths of the four pieces.

68. A washer and dryer combination is marked down from $720 to $583.20. What was the percent markdown?

69. In an account valued at $53,900, Phyllis Ophical has 500 shares of stock. Some shares are in Big Brother and the Holding Company, valued at $115 per share, and the rest are in Getridge Quick Corp., valued at $97 per share. How many shares of each are in the account?

70. A farmer needs 620 yards of fencing to enclose a rectangular pasture. The pasture borders on a river, so that one side doesn't need a fence. The one side parallel to the river is twice as long as the two sides perpendicular to the river. What are the dimensions of the pasture?

71. Jim and Bob sit at opposite ends of an 18-foot seesaw, with the fulcrum at its center. Jim weighs 160 pounds, and Bob weighs 200 pounds. If Kim sits 4 feet in front of Jim, the seesaw will balance. How much does Kim weigh?

72. If one number is three times as large as a second number, and x represents the second number, write an expression for five times the reciprocal of the first number.

73. Gus Undhite got a 5% pay raise. His new weekly pay was $20 more than it had been before. What was the amount of his new weekly pay?

74. The following is part of a will for someone with three children. "I leave twice as much money to my oldest child as to my youngest child. The middle child should receive $5,500 more than the youngest. The total to be divided is $87,500." How much money will each child receive?

75. You find the locker in your high school padlocked by your math teacher. There is a note: "In the combination to this lock, the first number is eight more than six times the second. The third number is twenty less than the sum of the first two. Furthermore, the sum of the numbers is 66. Find the numbers, and you can skip tomorrow's test." What is the combination?

76. For a concert, student tickets were $2 each and adult tickets were $4 each. If 200 tickets were sold and the total receipts were $750, how many student tickets were sold?

77. One car leaves San Francisco headed for Portland, a distance of 646 miles. At the same time, a second car leaves Portland headed toward San Francisco. If the first car averages 51 miles per hour and the second car averages 57 miles per hour, how long will it take the cars to meet?

78. A cyclist leaves Colorado Springs riding at the rate of 15 miles per hour. One hour later, a car leaves Colorado Springs going 60 miles per hour in the same direction. How long will it take the car to overtake the cyclist?

79. Two marathon runners begin a race at the same time, one running 12 miles per hour and one running 10 miles per hour. How long will it take before the two runners are $\frac{1}{4}$ of a mile apart?

80. A batch of mixed nuts is made to sell for $4.71 per pound. If 28 pounds of a cheaper mixture, selling for $3.50 per pound, are used along with 38 pounds of a more expensive mixture, what was the price per pound of the more expensive mixture?

81. How much plain water should be added to 6 gallons of a 15% alcohol solution in order to dilute it to a 10% solution?

82. A store sells a book for $57.68. The store marks up the price by 12% over the publisher's price on each book. How much did each book cost the store?

83. A jar contains $4.75 in quarters, dimes, and nickels. There are 40 coins in all. There are five more quarters than dimes. Find the number of quarters, dimes, and nickels.

84. A company uses the equation $V = C - 6500t$ to determine the depreciated value, V, after t years, of a machine which originally cost C dollars. A milling machine originally cost $110,000. In how many years will the depreciated value be $54,750?

85. Two painters who work at the same rate are working on a job. After they work together for 10 hours, one of the painters quits. The second painter requires 20 more hours to complete the job. How long would it have taken one of the painters, working alone, to do the entire job?

86. A telephone company estimates that the number N of phone calls per day between two cities with populations P_1 and P_2, which are d miles apart, is given by the formula

$$N = \frac{0.251 P_1 P_2}{d^2}$$

(a) If two cities are 75 miles apart, and their populations are 60,000 and 85,000, about how many phone calls would we expect per day between the two cities?

(b) Suppose there are about 10,000 calls per day between Dripping Faucet and Stench Lake, and that Dripping Faucet has a population of 125,000, and that the two cities are 800 miles apart. What is the approximate population of Stench Lake?

87. Three different-sized pipes feed water into a swimming pool. If the pipes can fill the pool individually in 6 hours, 10 hours, and 9 hours, how long will it take to fill the pool if all three pipes are open?

88. A pool has two pipes pumping water in, and one drainpipe. One of the two pipes feeding water in can fill the pool in 10 hours all by itself, and the other can fill the pool in 8 hours. It takes the drainpipe 13 hours to empty the pool. If the pool starts off empty, and all three pipes are left open, how long will it take the pool to fill?

89. On a trip from Pepper Pond City to Big Pebble, Mrs. Smith drove at an average speed of 62 mph. Returning, her average speed was 51 mph, and it took her 20 minutes longer. How far is Pepper Pond City from Big Pebble?

90. A two-digit number is nine more than the number you would get by reversing the digits. The second digit is one sixteenth of the number itself. What is the number?

91. If you reverse the digits of a particular three-digit number, you get exactly the same number you started with. The sum of the three digits is 13, and the number itself is seven more than 66 times as big as the sum of the last two digits. What is the number?

92. Neil Down rode a bicycle to a repair shop and then walked home. Neil averaged 14 mph riding and 3.5 mph walking. The round trip took 32 minutes. How far is it between Neal's home and the bicycle shop?

93. A parade 2 miles long is proceeding at 2.5 mph. How long will it take a runner, jogging at 7 mph, to travel from the front of the parade to the end of the parade?

94. A parade 2 miles long is proceeding at 2.5 mph. How long will it take a runner, jogging at 7 mph, to travel from the end of the parade to the front of the parade?

95. Two birds flew from the tops of two towers, 50 feet apart, flying at the same rate and beginning at the same time. One tower, however, is 30 feet high and the other tower is 40 feet high. They reach the same spot on the ground, simultaneously. How far is that spot on the ground from the foot of the 40-foot tower?

96. Ben Anna is 4 times as old as Ray Beeze. In 3 years Ben will be 3 times as old as Ray will be. How old is each now?

97. Matsuko is twice as old as her daughter Kazuko. Ten years ago, the sum of their ages was 31 years. How old is each person now?

98. Gail Bladder is now 29 years old and Clem Chowder is 17 years old. How long ago was Gail three times as old as Clem?

99. Eve Ann Jelical is twice as old as Dee Funct. If Eve were 6 years older and Dee were 9 years younger, Eve would be three times as old as Dee. How old are they?

100. The length of a rectangle is three times its width. If the perimeter of the rectangle is 24 feet, find the area.

101. The length of a rectangle is 11 meters more than the width. If the width is increased by 2 meters and the length is decreased by 5 meters, the area would remain the same. Find the original dimensions of the rectangle.

102. The first angle of a triangle is twice the second, and the third angle is 40° smaller than the second. Find the three angles.

103. The area of a triangle is 96 square inches, and the height is 8 inches. What is the length of the base?

104. Dinah Myte put 48% of her money in a 3.5% interest-bearing account, 32% in an account which returned 5% interest, and 20% in a higher-risk account whose value grew by 11.5% the first year. If her total return from the investments that first year was $1,562.40, find the total amount invested.

105. A goldsmith mixed 10 grams of a 50% gold alloy with 40 grams of a 15% gold alloy. What is the percent of gold in the resulting mixture?

106. How much water must evaporate from 8 quarts of a 55% antifreeze solution in order to bring the concentration to 80%?

107. A radiator contains 6 quarts of 30% antifreeze solution. How much should be drained and replaced with pure antifreeze in order to get a 50% antifreeze solution?

108. A piece of pipe is 26 feet long. The pipe must be cut so that one piece is 4 feet shorter than the other. What are the lengths of the two pieces after it is cut?

109. A clothing store sells suits at $185 and $235 each. The store sold 40 suits for a total of $8,000. How many of each type of suit did they sell?

110. When two batteries were connected in series, the total voltage was 65 volts. When they were connected in opposition, the resulting voltage was 17 volts. What were the voltages of the two batteries separately?

111. An airplane can fly at 385 mph with the wind and 321 mph against the wind. What is the speed of the airplane in still air, and what is the speed of the wind?

112. A cyclist and a pedestrian are 25 miles apart. If they travel toward each other, they will meet in one hour and 43 minutes. On the other hand, if the pedestrian travels in the opposite direction and the cyclist follows, the cyclist will overtake the pedestrian in 3 hours and 20 minutes. What are their speeds in miles per hour?

113. A screwdriver 9 inches long is used as a lever to open a can of paint. The tip of the screwdriver is placed under the lip of the can, with a fulcrum 0.18 inch from the tip. A force of 22 lb. is applied downward at the handle end of the screwdriver. What is the upward force exerted by the tip of the screwdriver on the lid?

114. In preparation for a stunt, two acrobats are standing on a plank 22 feet long. One acrobat weighs 130 lb. and the other weighs 156 lb. How far from the 130-lb. acrobat must the fulcrum be placed so that the two acrobats are balanced on the plank?

115. The fixed cost for making a bunch of television sets is $30,030. In addition, it costs $168 to make each set. The sets sell for $259 each. How many sets must be sold in order to break even?

116. What number must be added to both the numerator and denominator of the fraction $\frac{1}{5}$ in order to get a fraction equal to $\frac{8}{9}$?

117. The area of a rectangle is 208 square inches. The perimeter is 58 inches. What are the dimensions?

118. Two planes leave an airport at the same time and head for another airport 1,120 miles away. The speed of the first plane is $1\frac{1}{2}$ times the speed of the second plane. The second plane arrives 1 hour and 10 minutes after the first plane. What is the speed of the faster plane?

119. In a given electrical circuit, the relationship between I (current measured in amperes), E (voltage), and R (resistance in ohms) is given by

$$I^2R + IE = 8,000$$

Find I when $R = 4$ and $E = 100$. Assume $I > 0$.

120. A manufacturer finds that the total cost C of manufacturing and delivering x washing machines is expressed by

$$C = .01x^2 + 215x + 300,000$$

and that the devices can be sold for $364 each. How many machines does the manufacturer have to sell in order to break even?

121. If a stone is thrown upward at 96 feet per second, how long will it take to climb 80 feet high?

122. If a stone is thrown upward at 96 feet per second, how long will it be before it reaches its peak and then descends to a height of 80 feet on the way *down*?

123. A trapezoid has an area of 96 square inches. Its height is 16 inches, and one of its bases is 9 inches. How long is the other base?

124. If a frustrated computer user drops a PC out a window (with no initial *downward* velocity) on the top floor of a 600-foot building, how long will it take to hit the ground?

125. The demand equation for a specific commodity is given by

$$D = 855 - 300p$$

where D is the number of units demanded by consumers when the price p is dollars per unit. The supply equation, giving the number of units which producers are willing to supply at a price of p dollars per unit, is

$$S = 2,200p - 20$$

What is the equilibrium price?

126. What are the dimensions of a rectangle whose length is 2.5 times the width, and whose diagonal is $7\sqrt{29}$ (about 37.7)?

127. An aircraft flies for 200 miles in still air and then flies 150 miles into a 25-mph headwind. The second part of the trip takes 6 minutes less than the first 200 miles. How long does the entire trip take?

128. Ann Onimous sells 2 TV's and 5 VCR's for $2,953. The next day, she sells 4 TV's and 2 VCR's for $3,034. How much does each cost?

129. A circular lawn is surrounded by a circular sidewalk 2 feet wide. The total area of the sidewalk is approximately 515.22 square feet. What is the diameter of the lawn (not including the sidewalk)?

130. A car travels 50 miles in the same time that a plane travels 250 miles. The plane is 248 mph faster than the car. What is the speed of the car?

131. Paul Bearer is the manager of a computer store. He knows that fixed costs are $9,040 per month and that unit costs are $1,210 for each computer sold. The store can sell the computers for $1,775 each. How many computers must be sold for the store to break even?

132. A sales clerk can choose from two salary options: Either a straight 7.5% commission, or a salary of $200 per week plus a 2.5% commission. How much would the clerk have to sell each week in order for the two salary plans to come out the same?

133. An angle is 46° larger than its complement. Find the angle.

134. An angle is 38° smaller than its supplement. Find the angle.

135. One square has sides of 10 inches, and a second square has sides of 5 inches. What is the ratio of the **area** of the first square to the **area** of the second square?

136. One cup (8 fluid ounces) of water was taken as a sample from a 12-gallon container. The cup of water contained 0.3 ounce of salt. About how much salt was in the 12 gallons?

137. Otto Biography and Lee K. Fawcett caught 62 fish in a pond, tagged them, and then released them. A month later, they caught 75 fish and found that 13 of them were tagged. Estimate the number of fish in the pond.

138. A flagpole casts a shadow 20 feet long at the same time that Ben Dover (who is 6 feet tall) casts a shadow 3.75 feet long. How tall is the flagpole?

139. The number of calories required daily in order to maintain a constant body weight varies directly with the person's weight. If 2,100 calories per day are required to maintain a weight of 160 lb., how many calories per day are required to maintain a weight of 185 lb.?

140. The length of time it takes to do a job varies inversely with the number of people working. If it takes four people 9 hours to do a job, how long will it take seven people to do it?

141. The length of time it takes to wrap all the Christmas presents varies directly with the number of presents and inversely with the number of people doing the wrapping. It takes two people 2 hours to wrap 80 gifts. If 130 gifts must be wrapped in $\frac{1}{2}$ hour, how many people are needed?

142. The daily number of phone calls between two cities varies jointly with the populations of the two cities, and inversely with the **square** of the distance between the cities. Dweebville has a population of 60,000 and Dork Springs has a population of 75,000. The two cities are 45 miles apart, and there are approximately 100,000 phone calls between the two cities every day.

   (a) Adver City, 85 miles from Dweebville, has a population of 8,500 people. About how many phone calls are there between Dweebville and Adver City?

   (b) Diver City is 150 miles from Dork Springs, and there are about 262,500 phone calls per day between the two cities. What is the population of Diver City?

   (c) Simpli City has a population of 1,250 people, and there are 3,750 calls per day between Simpli City and Dweebville. How far is Simpli City from Dweebville?

143. A basketball team scored 89 points with one-point free throws, two-point field goals, and three-point baskets. The number of two-point field goals was 4 more than the number of free throws. If there had been one more free throw, the number of free throws would have been six times the number of three-pointers. How many three-pointers were made?

144. A rectangle is to be drawn so that the ratio of the length to the width is 3.5 to 1. The perimeter of the rectangle is to be 33 feet. What are the dimensions of the rectangle?

145. A suit which normally sells for $260 is marked down to $215.80. What is the percent discount?

146. A washing machine has been discounted by 19%, and now is priced at $339.39. What was the original price?

147. A box of Christmas cards is being sold at a 65% discount the day after Christmas. If the original price of the box was $13.80, what is the new discounted price?

148. A store buys tires from the manufacturer for $36.22 each, and sells them for $41.65 each. What is the percentage markup in price?

149. A stone is dropped into a well. The splash is heard exactly 2 seconds later. How far is the water below the surface of the earth?

150. During one month, Helen Hiwater used 1,100 units of electricity and 600 units of gas, for a total cost of $116.60. The next month, she used 900 units of electricity and 700 units of gas, for a total cost of $106.90. What is the unit cost of electricity?

151. Two trains, 451 miles apart, start traveling toward each other at noon. Their average rates of speed are 56 mph and 76 mph. What time will it be when they pass each other?

152. A train leaves the station at 2:00 PM, traveling 60 mph. A second train leaves at 3:30 PM, traveling at 75 mph in the same direction. How far will the second train have to go before it catches up to the first train?

153. Cora Nary rides her bike to school at an average rate of 12 mph. If she drives instead, she drives at 40 mph and arrives 21 minutes sooner than when she rides her bike. How far is it to school?

The remaining problems require (or at least greatly benefit from) a knowledge of exponential and/or logarithmic functions.

154. If $1,200 is placed in account which pays $5\frac{1}{2}$% interest, compounded monthly, how long will it take for the value of the account to reach $2,000?

155. If $1,200 is placed in an account which pays $5\frac{1}{2}$% interest, compounded monthly, what will the value of the account be seven years later?

156. How much money must be deposited into an account which pays 6% interest (compounded annually), in order to have $200,000 six years from now?

157. Dick Shenary put $11,000 into an account in which interest and dividends were paid into the account quarterly. In 5 years he had $20,000. What was the annual rate of return?

158. How many years will it take an investment to double if the interest rate is 6% and the interest is compounded annually?

159. The population of San Antonio was 588,000 in 1960, and 633,000 in 1967. Find the formula for estimating the population of San Antonio t years after 1960, and estimate the population in 1990.

160. The population of East Haircut was 5,100 in 1,980, and 5,950 in 1990. How long will it take for the population to double?

161. The half-life of barfium is 29.3 days. How much of a 19-gram sample is left after 50 days?

162. A 50-gram sample of geekium decayed down to 40 grams in 93 years. What is the half-life, to the nearest full year?

163. When a living organism dies, it takes in no more carbon, and the existing carbon-14 in the body begins to decay steadily with a half-life of 5,750 years. How old is a fossil which has lost 54.87% of its carbon-14?

164. Students forget material they have learned in a math class according to the formula:
$$S(t) = S(0) - k\log(t+1)$$

Where $S(t)$ is the score on a comprehensive exam t months after the end of the course, and k is a constant which varies from person to person and from class to class. If Anne Thrax scored 89 on the original final exam and then scored 54 seven months later, what is her predicted score on an exam a year after the class ended?

165. If an algebra book cost $20 in 1968 and $48.50 in 1995, how much will it cost in 2001? (Assume the price increases exponentially.)

 Useful Facts and Formulas

While this Appendix is not intended to provide an exhaustive and complete list of all facts and formulas you need in any word problem you might ever encounter, these should be enough to get you through almost every problem in this book, and most problems in other books as well.

 Perimeters

Rectangle: $P = 2l + 2w$, where l = length and w = width.

Square: $P = 4s$, where s = the length of one side.

Triangle: $P = a + b + c$, where a, b, and c are the lengths of the sides.

For any polygon in general, the perimeter is the sum of the lengths of the sides.

Circle: $C = 2\pi r = \pi d$, where r = radius, and d = diameter. (For circles, the perimeter is usually called the *circumference*.)

 Areas

Rectangle: $A = lw$, where l and w are the length and width of the rectangle.

Square: $A = s^2$, where s = the length of a side.

Triangle: $A = \frac{1}{2}bh$, where b = the base, and h = height (sometimes also called the *altitude*).

Trapezoid: $A = \frac{b_1+b_2}{2}(h)$, where b_1 and b_2 are the bases, and h = height.

Circle: $A = \pi r^2$, where r = radius.

Cylinder (surface area): $A = 2\pi rh + 2\pi r^2 = 2\pi r(r + h)$, where r = radius, and h = height.

Sphere (surface area): $A = 4\pi r^2$, where r = radius.

Rectangular box (surface area): $A = 2(lw + wh + lh)$, where l = length, w = width, and h = height.

Cone (total surface area including base): $A = \pi r^2 + \pi r \sqrt{r^2 + h^2}$, where r = radius of the base, and h = height (from the center of the base to the vertex).

 ## Volumes

Rectangular box: $V = lwh$, where l = length, w = width, and h = height.

Sphere: $V = \frac{4}{3}\pi r^3$, where r = radius.

Cone: $V = \frac{1}{3}\pi r^2 h$, where r = radius, and h = height.

 ## Miscellaneous Geometric Facts

The three angles in any triangle total to exactly 180°.

Pythagorean Theorem:

> For *right* triangles, $a^2 + b^2 = c^2$, where a and b are the lengths of the legs, and c is the length of the hypotenuse.

An *isosceles* triangle is one in which two of the three sides are equal to each other. In such cases, a straight line drawn from the vertex between the two equal sides, perpendicular to the third side, will bisect *both* that third side *and* the angle at the vertex between the two equal sides.

An *equilateral* triangle is one in which all three sides are equal. All three angles of an equilateral triangle are equal to 60°.

Two *complementary* angles add up to 90°.

Two *supplementary* angles add up to 180°.

When two straight lines cross, the angles on opposite sides of the intersection are equal. (For some unfathomable reason, such angles are called *vertical* angles. They have nothing whatsoever to do with verticalness.)

The *dimensions* of a rectangle are the length and the width.

The opposite angles of a parallelogram are equal.

Two adjacent (or *consecutive*) angles of a parallelogram add up to 180°.

If two triangles are *similar*, it means that the ratios of all three pairs of corresponding sides are equal. For example, the two triangles are similar. In that similarity relationship, side A corresponds to x, B corresponds to y, and C corresponds to z.

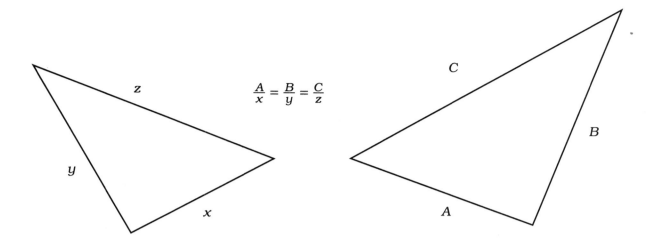

$$\frac{A}{x} = \frac{B}{y} = \frac{C}{z}$$

 Levers

To find out whether a lever (such as a see saw) is in balance, multiply each force on the lever by the distance between the fulcrum and the point at which that force is applied. Then add up those products for all forces on one side of the lever, and add up the products for all forces on the other side. If those sums are equal, the lever is in balance.

Similarly, if a downward force D is being exerted at one end of a lever, there is an upward force U exerted by the other end. If x is the distance from the downward force to the fulcrum, and y is the distance between the fulcrum and the upward force, then $Dx = Uy$.

Example:

A weight of 20 lb. at 36 inches from the fulcrum, and a weight of 25 lb. at 30 inches from the fulcrum on the same side, are in balance with a weight of 35 lb. at 42 inches from the fulcrum on the other side, because:

$$(20 \cdot 36) + (25 \cdot 30) = 1,470 = 35 \cdot 42$$

Maximum/Minimum Value of a Quadratic

The largest or smallest possible value of a quadratic expression

$$ax^2 + bx + c$$

occurs when $x = \frac{-b}{2a}$. The maximum or minimum value itself is found by substituting $x = \frac{-b}{2a}$ into the original quadratic expression. If a is a negative number, then the value is the maximum value for the expression; if a is positive, then the value is the minimum possible value. (Any quadratic expression has either a minimum value or a maximum value, but not both.)

Rising and Falling Objects

The formula:

$$h = h_0 + v_0 t - 16t^2$$

describes the height of an object which is thrown up or down (or dropped), and which has no additional force other than gravity being applied to it. The variables are:

h_0 = the original height of the object
v_0 = original velocity (positive if upward, negative if downward, 0 if the object was dropped)
t = time in seconds following the original throw or drop

Profit

The profit of any enterprise is equal to the income (which is often mostly sales) minus the expenses (which include the cost of manufacturing and selling, and the amount paid by the seller for the original materials or items to be sold).

Interest

Simple interest: The formula for simple interest (interest which is computed on the amount of principal only, and is paid only once at the end of the period in question), is:

$$I = Prt$$

where I = amount of interest
P = the original principal amount
r = interest rate (remember that 5.5%, for example, must be converted to .055)
t = length of time, measured in years (assuming that r is an annual interest rate)

Compound interest: The formula for interest which is computed on the sum of the principal plus the accrued interest, and is paid at the end of each compounding period, is:

$$P = P_0\left(1 + \frac{r}{n}\right)^{nt}$$
$$\text{or } I = P_0\left[\left(1+\frac{r}{n}\right)^{nt} - 1\right]$$

where P = the new value of the account after interest has been added
P_0 = the original principal amount
r = interest rate (remember that 5.5%, for example, must be converted to .055)

n = number of compounding periods per year
(monthly = 12, quarterly = 4, etc.)
t = length of time, measured in years (assuming that r is
an annual interest rate)
I = amount of interest

A Few Comments about Fractions

Yes, you were promised that there would be no pure math in this book. But fractions are such a stumbling block for so many students, and there are so many misconceptions about how fractions should be handled, that it is important to present some basic facts.

1. Fractions can be multiplied by multiplying the tops and bottoms straight across:
$$\frac{3}{x} \cdot \frac{5}{11} = \frac{15}{11x}$$

2. Fractions are divided by turning the second fraction upside down, and then multiplying:
$$\frac{3}{x} \div \frac{5}{11} = \frac{3}{x} \cdot \frac{11}{5} = \frac{33}{5x}$$

3. When you multiply a fraction by whole number (or a non-fractional algebraic expression), it is only the *numerator* (the top) that gets multiplied. The denominator (bottom) is left alone.
$$5 \cdot \frac{3}{4} = \frac{15}{4} \qquad \left(\text{not } \frac{15}{20}!\right)$$

$$(x-1) \cdot \frac{2}{7} = \frac{2x-2}{7} \qquad \left(\text{not } \frac{2x-2}{7x-7}!\right)$$

4. It is not legal for a denominator to be equal to zero. The fraction $\frac{3x}{x-6}$ is undefined when $x = 6$. (It's perfectly OK for x to be zero as long as that doesn't make the denominator zero.

5. It *is* legal for the *numerator* of a fraction to be zero (as long as the denominator isn't zero too). If the numerator is zero, then the fraction is equal to zero no matter what the denominator is: $\frac{0}{5} = 0$.
$\frac{x-3}{x+2} = 0$ when $x = 3$. $\frac{0}{x+2} = 0$ as long as x isn't –2.

Three Lies about Fractions

Lie Number 1:

> *A numerical fraction whose numerator is larger than the denominator is "improper."*

Fact: There is absolutely nothing "improper" about the fraction $\frac{3}{2}$; in fact, for almost all mathematical purposes, $\frac{3}{2}$ is a much easier number to work

116

with than $1\frac{1}{2}$. **Remove the word "improper" from your vocabulary when it comes to fractions!**

Lie Number 2:

> *There is something wrong with a fraction if it isn't in lowest terms.*

Fact: This is like saying that *General* Washington was not the first president of the U.S. because the right answer is *George* Washington. If $\frac{1}{2}$ is the right answer to a problem, then $\frac{3}{6}$ absolutely *has* to be right also—because $\frac{1}{2}$ and $\frac{3}{6}$ are the very same number! Reducing fractions to lowest terms is entirely a question of style, not of mathematical correctness.

Lie Number 3:

> *In order to add or subtract two fractions, you must first find the least common denominator.*

Fact: In all of mathematics, there is no lie which has done as much damage to the mathematical careers of students as this one has. Here are the *true* facts:

1. In order to add or subtract two fractions, they must have the same denominator. There is no exception to this rule. (This "same denominator" can also be called a "common denominator," but it most emphatically does *not* have to be the *least* common denominator. And contrary to what you have probably been told, a *common* denominator is very easy to find—see below.)

2. It is always allowed to multiply the top and bottom of any fraction by the same thing, as long as that thing is not equal to zero.

So here are the procedures for adding or subtracting fractions:

If two fractions already have the same denominator, we can add or subtract them by just adding or subtracting their numerators, and leaving the denominator alone:

$$\frac{5}{x} + \frac{3}{x} = \frac{8}{x}$$
$$\frac{5}{x} - \frac{3}{x} = \frac{2}{x}$$
$$\frac{5}{x} - \frac{x+1}{x} = \frac{5-(x+1)}{x} = \frac{4-x}{x}$$

If two fractions do NOT already have the same denominator, **you can always get them to have the same denominator by multiplying the top and bottom of each fraction by the denominator of the <u>other</u> fraction.**

An example will serve to illustrate:

● Add $\frac{2}{3} + \frac{1}{4}$.

SOLUTION: Multiply the top and bottom of $\frac{2}{3}$ by 4 (the denominator of $\frac{1}{4}$), and multiply the top and bottom of $\frac{1}{4}$ by 3 (the denominator of $\frac{2}{3}$):

$$\left(\frac{2}{3}\right)\left(\frac{4}{4}\right) + \left(\frac{1}{4}\right)\left(\frac{3}{3}\right)$$
$$= \frac{8}{12} + \frac{3}{12}$$
$$= \frac{11}{12}$$

Does this always work? Yes. Every single time, without exception.

Even with fractions that have x's? Yes.

Another example will serve to illustrate:

● Subtract: $\frac{x}{3} - \frac{4x}{x-5}$

SOLUTION: We multiply the top and bottom of the first fraction by $x-5$, the denominator of the second fraction. We multiply the top and bottom of the second fraction by 3, the denominator of the first fraction:

$$\left(\frac{x}{3}\right)\left(\frac{x-5}{x-5}\right) - \left(\frac{4x}{x-5}\right)\left(\frac{3}{3}\right)$$
$$= \frac{x^2-5x}{3x-15} - \frac{12x}{3x-15}$$
$$= \frac{x^2-17x}{3x-15}$$

It's just that simple.

When adding or subtracting three or more fractions, we do the operations one at a time from left to right. In these cases it is always a good idea to check after each additional step to see whether any of the fractions can be reduced before going on:

$$\frac{3}{A} - \frac{2}{3A} + \frac{5}{6}$$

First we multiply the top and bottom of the first fraction by $3A$, and the top and bottom of the second fraction by A (**see note on next page), and then add:

$$\left(\frac{3}{A}\right)\left(\frac{3A}{3A}\right) - \left(\frac{2}{3A}\right)\left(\frac{A}{A}\right) + \left(\frac{5}{6}\right)$$
$$= \frac{9A}{3A^2} - \frac{2A}{3A^2} + \frac{5}{6}$$
$$= \frac{7A}{3A^2} + \frac{5}{6}$$
$$= \frac{7}{3A} + \frac{5}{6}$$

(The last step came from dividing an A out of the top and bottom of $\frac{7A}{3A^2}$.)

Now we do the remaining addition by multiplying the top and bottom of the first fraction by 6, and the top and bottom of the second fraction by $3A$:

$$\left(\frac{7}{3A}\right)\left(\frac{6}{6}\right) + \left(\frac{5}{6}\right)\left(\frac{3A}{3A}\right)$$
$$= \frac{42}{18A} + \frac{15A}{18A}$$
$$= \frac{42+15A}{18A}$$
$$= \frac{14+5A}{6A}$$

The last step (dividing 3 out of the top and bottom) was unnecessary, of course; $\frac{42+15A}{18A}$ is a perfectly good answer.

**NOTE: Of course we could just multiply the top and bottom of $\frac{3}{A}$ by 3, giving both fractions a denominator of $3A$. If you notice that possibility, it is definitely an easier method. The important point here is that the method we used always works, even in those (comparatively rare!) cases where there is an easier alternative.

Unit Equivalents

Here are some of the most common equivalents which come in handy when problems deal in more than one unit of measurement:

1 mile = 5,280 feet = 1,760 yards = 1,609.3 meters = 1.6093 kilometers
1 foot = 12 inches = .3048 meter
1 yard = 3 feet
1 meter = 39.37 inches = 3.28 feet
1 inch = 2.54 centimeters

1 degree = $\frac{\pi}{180}$ (about 0.0175) radian

1 radian = $\frac{180}{\pi}$ (about 57.3) degrees

1 pound = 16 ounces = 0.454 kilogram
1 ounce = 0.02835 kilogram = 28.35 grams
1 kilogram = 2.2 pounds
1 gram = 0.035 ounce

1 gallon = 4 quarts
1 quart = 2 pints = 0.946 liter
1 pint = 2 cups = 16 fluid ounces
1 cup = 8 fluid ounces
1 liter = 1.057 quarts

Formulas for converting between Celsius temperatures (C) and Fahrenheit temperatures (F):

$$F = \frac{9}{5}C + 32$$

$$C = \frac{5}{9}(F - 32)$$

 A Suggestion about Studying for Exams

You studied hard for your math test. You did dozens of problems (it seemed like hundreds, but it probably wasn't.) You knew how to do every type of problem that could possibly be on the test. You were really ready for this one.

But you bombed the test. What happened?

There are many reasons this could happen—test anxiety, lack of sleep, etc. But there is one common reason which not too many people think of. When you prepare for a test, you do 12 problems in a row from, let's say, one section of Chapter 3. By the time you do the 12th problem, you know the drill perfectly. After all, the 12th problem is almost exactly like the previous 11 except for a few numbers changed here and there. So now you've conquered that section, and you go on to another section to do the same thing.

Now you arrive for your test. You open it up, and there are 20 problems. There is no indication of which section of the book problem #6 is from. Problem #12 bears no resemblance whatsoever to problem #11 or problem #13. You will have to do problem #3 *without* the benefit of having just done 8 similar problems just before #3. You are at sea, with none of the familiar landmarks to guide you.

The fact is that while you were studying, even if you didn't look at your notes or the answers in the back of the book, you had the benefit of LOTS of hints. You knew which chapter you were in; which section of which chapter; you had fallen into a step-by-step drill for problems from that section; and you were able to do those problems almost automatically. But you never developed *the ability to identify what kind of problem you had in the first place*.

So here is a suggestion for preparing for math exams: Copy several problems from each section of the book which will be covered on the exam. Put each problem on a separate sheet of paper or index card. DO NOT write down the section or page that the problem came from (if you want to keep track of where the problem came from, write that information on the back). Now shuffle the problems into a random order, and then try to solve them without referring to the book. You'll be amazed at how hard it is! You will not only be learning how to do each type of problem, but also *learning to identify what kind of problem it is*.

THIS WILL HELP! DO IT! Yes, it's time-consuming, but DO IT!!

Chapter 1

Exercise A, page 9.

1. Obvious answer: between 0% and 100%. A better answer: somewhere between 0 and 10%. (The price was reduced by $2,000. If it had been reduced by 10%, it would have gone down by $2,400.)

2. Obvious answer: between 0 and 60 inches. A better answer: between 6 inches (because they have to be 6 inches longer than the shortest piece) and 30 inches (since there are two equal pieces which come from a 60-inch board, they can't be more than 30 inches).

3. Obvious answer: between 0 and 52. A better answer: between 27 and 52. (Since Sally is older, her age must account for more than half the sum of her age and her daughter's age.)

4. Your answer will depend on how much calculation you want to do. But you can certainly say that the speed was more than 45 mph, and certainly less than 145 mph.

5. Obvious answer: between 0 and 75 for each. A better answer: the possible range of values for the nickels is 38 to 75, and for the dimes 0 to 37. (If they were all dimes, the value would be $7.50. If they were all nickels, the value would be $3.75. The given value, $4.75, is closer to $3.75 than to $7.50, so it's a good bet that more than half of the coins are nickels.)

6. She must have driven more than 100 miles, because for 100 miles the cost would be $39.50 plus 100×27¢, or $39.50 + $27.00, which is $66.50. On the other hand, she didn't drive much more than 100 miles, because her total cost was only a little more than $66.50. So perhaps we could say between 100 and 200 miles.

7. Obvious answer: between 0 and 10. A better answer: between 0 and 8. (The student got 90% of the 40 multiple-choice and short-answer questions right. Since the true-false questions lowered his score to 82%, he must have gotten fewer than 90% of them right.)

8. We know she bought at least one 16-ounce container. But since she also bought at least one 32-ounce and one 12-ounce, that leaves a maximum of 324 − 32 − 12 = 280 ounces for 16-ounce containers. Since 280 ÷ 16 is less than 18, the answer has to be between 1 and 18.

9. If Ray worked exactly as fast as Letitia, the two of them would finish the job in one hour. Since they do it faster than that, Ray must be faster than Letitia. So the answer for Ray must be between 1 and 2 hours.

10. Obvious answer: between 0° and 180°. A better answer: between 40° and 90°. (In this case, the largest angle is only 40° larger than the smallest. The largest angle couldn't be 90°, because then there would have to be two other angles of at least 50°. But 50° + 50° + 90° = 190°, and that's too much. On the other hand, if the largest angle is 40° larger than the smallest, then certainly the largest angle is at least 40°. Actually we can do even better than that, but this is good enough.)

Chapter 2

Exercise A, page 14.

The three times are the time it takes Otto to paint the house alone, the time it takes Adam to paint the house alone, and the time it takes Otto and Adam working together to paint the house.

Exercise B, page 14.

The three quantities are the first integer, the second integer, and the third integer. It MUST be specified which variable applies to which integer! So we set up the variables:

x = first integer
y = second integer
z = third integer

Exercise C, page 15.

Jack Spratt's weight is 85 pounds more than his wife's weight. The sum of their weights is 395 pounds. How much does Jack weigh alone? The variables are then:

J = Jack Spratt's weight
W = his wife's weight

Exercise D, page 17.

The other two quantities are the total cost of the adult tickets and the total cost of the children's tickets. It would probably be confusing to say "total adult ticket sales," etc., because that phrase could refer either to the number of tickets *or* to their cost.

Exercise E, page 18.

The other two quantities are the total value of the $6.00-per-lb. nuts and the total value of the $4.50-per-lb. nuts.

Exercise F, page 19.

The unknown quantities are:
- The amount of 10% pesticide solution to be used.
- The total amount of the final mixture.
- The amount of pure pesticide in the 10% pesticide solution used.
- The amount of pure pesticide in the final mixture.

Exercise G, page 21.

$V = 350$
$l = l$ (we can use l because there's only one length in the problem)
$w = l$ (since it's a square base, l and w are the same)
$h = 14$

Exercise H, page 28.

For the first occurrence of the formula $Q = Q_0 e^{kt}$:

$Q = 2$
$Q_0 = 1$
k = unknown
$t = 55$

For the second occurrence:

Q = unknown
$Q_0 = 87,000$
k = unknown (but will be known when first occurrence of formula is solved)
$t = 36$

Exercise I, pages 31-32.

1. a = the *amount* of the reduction
   b = the new price

2. k = the constant of variation (to use the formula $y = k\frac{x}{z}$ when y varies directly with x and inversely with z)
   a = the length of time it takes 7 cooks to prepare a banquet for 175 people

3. a = the *amount* of interest
   b = the interest rate

4. a = the first digit of the original number
   b = the second digit of the original number
   c = the third digit of the original number
   d = the original number
   e = the number which results from reversing the digits of the original number

5. a = the number of cars
   b = the number of trucks
   c = the total in tolls paid by all the cars
   d = the total in tolls paid by all the trucks

6. a = Michael's age now
   b = Nick's age now
   c = Michael's age in 2 years
   d = Nick's age in 2 years

7. a = amount of 52% peanut mixture to use
   b = amount of 30% peanut mixture to use
   c = amount of peanuts in 52% mixture
   d = amount of peanuts in 30% mixture

8. a = Marian's rate (speed)
   b = Marian's distance
   c = George's distance
   x = Marian's time
   y = George's time
   (We can possibly get along without x and y, because the times for George and Marian can be easily and directly calculated from the given information. But the times weren't given explicitly, and since we will need the formula $rt = d$, it's a good idea to define variables for two times.)

9. a = original base
   c = original height
   d = base after change
   e = height after change
   (Note: we avoid using the letter b, because it stands for the base in the formula $A = \frac{1}{2}bh$.)

10. a = fraction of teacher's mind which Stan can drive him out of in 1 minute
    b = fraction of teacher's mind which Leonard can drive him out of in 1 minute
    c = fraction of teacher's mind which Stan and Leonard, working together, can drive him out of in 1 minute

11. a = number of copies which will be sold

b = number of copies in excess of 50 which will be sold

c = new price per book, after the price reduction

Chapter 3

Exercise A, page 33.

   a. $n - 2$

   b. $5n$

   c. $n - 18$

   d. $18 - n$

   e. $\frac{64}{n}$

   f. $\frac{64}{n}$

   g. $\frac{n}{64}$

Exercise B, page 34.

   a. $25 - \frac{x}{4}$

   b. $\frac{25}{x-4}$

   c. $17 + x^2$

   d. $\frac{17+x}{36-x}$

Exercise C, page 35.

$B - 3(23.79)$, or $B - 71.37$

Exercise D, page 36.

P = Peter's speed

$P + 4$ = George's speed

Exercise E, page 38.

$3.54

Exercise F, page 38.

P = number of pears,

$59P$ (or $.59P$) = total cost of pears

Exercise G, page 39.

C = cost of one tape

$11C$ = cost of 11 tapes

Exercise H, page 40.

$168 - C$

Exercise I, page 41.

   a. $0.1S$

   b. $S + 500$

   c. $0.045(S + 500)$, **or** $0.1S + .02(500)$

Exercise J, page 41.

With the wind: $250 + W$

Against the wind: $250 - W$

Exercise K, page 42.

First integer: x

Second integer: $x + 2$

Third integer: $x + 4$

Exercise L, page 43.

F = first digit

$11 - F$ = second digit

$10F + 11 - F = 9F + 11$ = original two-digit number

$10(11 - F) + F = 110 - 9F$ = number with digits reversed.

Exercise M, pages 49-50.

1. $x + 7$

2. $7 - x$ (NOT $x - 7$)

3. $\frac{7}{x}$

4. $8(x - 2)$ or $8x - 16$

5. $x + 11$

6. x = number of men

$12 - x$ = number of women

$180x$ = total weight of men

$145(12 - x)$ = total weight of women

           OR

x = number of women

$12 - x$ = number of men

$145x$ = total weight of women

$180(12 - x)$ = total weight of men

7. x = time taken by Scott to load the truck

$\frac{1}{x}$ = fraction of truck Scott can load alone in one hour

8. x = Karen's age now

$x - 15$ = Marsha's age now

$x - 12$ = Karen's age 12 years ago

$x - 27$ (or $x - 15 - 12$) = Marsha's age 12 years ago

9. $x = $ first digit

$10 - x = $ second digit

$10x + (10 - x) = 9x + 10 = $ the original two-digit number

$10(10 - x) + x = 100 - 9x = $ the number with the digits reversed

10. $x = $ cost of one calculator

$12x = $ cost of 12 calculators

11. $x = $ number of women

$35 - x = $ number of men

(or the other way around)

12. $x = $ distance from Middle Haircut to West Haircut

$190 - x$, or $1.5x = $ distance from Middle Haircut to East Haircut

13. $x = $ number of \$1.00 reductions from the original fee

$10x = $ number of additional members resulting from reduced fee

$10x + 2 = $ number of total members after fee is reduced

$35 - x = $ new membership fee

$(35 - x)(10x + 2) = $ total membership fees collected

14. $x = $ taxes paid last year

$1.15x = $ taxes paid this year

15. $x = $ first integer

$x + 2 = $ second integer

$x + 4 = $ third integer

16. $x = $ amount of water to be added

$0 = $ amount of okra juice in the water to be added

(None of the other quantities involve x at all; they are either given or can be immediately calculated.)

Chapter 4

Exercise A, page 53.

$x = $ first integer

$x + 2 = $ second integer

$x + 4 = $ third integer

Exercise B, page 53.

The quantities defined previously were:

$F = $ first digit

$11 - F = $ second digit

$10F + 11 - F = 9F + 11 = $ original two-digit number

$10(11 - F) + F = 110 - 9F = $ number with digits reversed

Equation : $110 - 9F = 9F + 11 - 45$

Solution: $F = 8$. Therefore the first digit is 8, the second digit is $11 - F = 3$, and the number we want is 83.

Exercise C, page 61.

The first equation should have been:

$$8,000 = \frac{(10,000)(20,000)}{25^2} k$$

The solution is $k = .025$.

The next occurrence of the formula should have looked like:

$$x = \frac{(435,000)(397,000)}{(260)^2}(.025)$$

The solution is about 63,867 phone calls per day.

Chapter 5

Exercise A, page 66.

In **minutes**:

$C = $ time taken by Carlos to type the document

$C + 20 = $ time taken by Ramon to type the document

$180 = $ time taken by both working together to type the document

$\frac{1}{C} = $ portion of the document typed by Carlos in 1 minute

$\frac{1}{C+20} = $ portion of the document typed by Ramon in 1 minute

$\frac{1}{180} = $ portion of the document typed by both working together in 1 minute

In **hours**:

$C = $ time taken by Carlos to type the document

$C + \frac{1}{3} = $ time taken by Ramon to type the document

$3 = $ time taken by both working together to type the document

$\frac{1}{C} = $ portion of the document typed by Carlos in 1 hour

$\frac{1}{C+\frac{1}{3}} = $ portion of the document typed by Ramon in 1 hour

$\frac{1}{3} = $ portion of the document typed by both working together in 1 hour

Exercise B, page 68.

8064 minutes.

Exercise C, page 68.

Approximately 46.53 kg per meter.

Exercise D, page 69.

1. About 9.47 mph
2. About 27.4 years
3. About 69.4 square feet
4. About 5.8 cubic feet
5. 18 quarters, 50 pennies
6. 1 hour $22\frac{1}{2}$ minutes studying, and 2 hours $7\frac{1}{2}$ minutes playing Nintendo
7. Kareem is 7 feet 2 inches, and Muggsy is 5 feet 4 inches.
8. 2 full crates and 20 boxes

Chapter 6

Exercise A, pages 77-78.

1. 10.95 inches
2. 11.5×17.5 miles
3. 172 square feet
4. 9.064 square feet
5. $\frac{1}{2}$ foot
6. 85 miles
7. 6 minutes

Chapter 7

Exercise A, page 80.

230 feet

Exercise B, page 82.

1.5 minutes $\left(\frac{1}{40}$ of an hour$\right)$

Exercise C, pages 84-85.

1. 549.7 feet (549 feet 8 inches)
2. 92.68 yards (92 yards 2 feet 1 inch)
3. 1.5 inches
4. 38.5°
5. 10.64 feet (10 feet 8 inches)
6. 20,586.5 miles
7. He will be tackled (just barely).
8. 15.7°
9. 2,000 feet
10. 2.75 minutes (0.04585 hour)

Chapter 8

Exercise A, page 90.

Use 12 inches for the square and 9.4248 inches for the circle.

Exercise B, page 94.

The point is (–1, –1).

Exercise C, page 95.

32 feet per second

Exercise D, page 97.

1.432 degrees per second

Exercise E, page 97.

.5 (or $\frac{1}{2}$) foot per second.

Exercise F, pages 97-98.

1. $12\sqrt{2}$, or about 16.97
2. 200
3. About (2.158, 4.658)
4. About 1.09 feet square (The equation has a second solution, but it would require us to cut out more than the entire width of the piece of cardboard.)
5. 120°
6. $\frac{2}{11}$ units per second
7. About 0.0116 inch/min
8. $\frac{160\pi}{3}$ (about 167.55) miles per minute, or about 2.793 miles per second
9. About 271.22 cubic feet per minute; exact figure is $4\pi\left(\frac{315}{\pi}\right)^{\frac{2}{3}}$
10. About 10.087 mph

Exercises

1. N = a number; $N – N + 2$, or 2
2. N = a number; $\frac{11}{15}N$
3. N = a number; $33N$
4. N = a number; $11N – 1$
5. N = a number; $N^2 – 6N – 12$
6. N = a number; $28N + 5$
7. x = smaller number; $x + 23$
   OR: x = larger number; $44 – x$
8. x = smaller number; $3x – 79$
   OR: x = larger number; $50 – 3x$
9. $26x$
10. $x + 193,969$
11. $A = 2B$; $C = 4B$

12. $12 - t$

13. 80, 81, and 82

14. −64, −62, −60

15. 10, 11, 12

16. 39, 41, 43

17. −80, −82, −84, −86

18. 52, 53, 54

19. 96, 97

20. 2, 3

21. 6, 8

22. 35, 37

23. 84, 85, 86, 87

24. 10, 12

25. 4.25%

26. 10.5%

27. 6.125%

28. 11

29. 7 feet

30. $\sqrt{16200}$ (or 127.28) feet

31. Train A: 24 mph; Train B: 10mph

32. $\sqrt{128}$ (11.3) seconds

33. $\frac{-5+\sqrt{2073}}{4}$ (or 10.1) seconds

34. 600 feet

35. $\sqrt{\frac{175}{16}}$ (or 3.3) seconds

36. 11 lots

37. $7.65

38. 48 feet

39. 89

40. 12

41. 22 and 40

42. 13 and 52

43. 16 and 23

44. 10, 12, and 14

45. 18 inches, 18 inches, and 3 inches

46. 42 feet and 28 feet

47. $4,000 at $7\frac{1}{2}$%; $14,000 at 9%

48. The 12% gain was on $13,500; the 15% loss was on $4,500

49. $14,000

50. 32 gallons of 30% alcohol; 48 gallons of 70% alcohol

51. 1875 gallons

52. $\frac{x}{4}$

53. 18.5% (approximate)

54. $127.50

55. 150

56. 39 and 65

57. I'm 24, Ray is 30.

58. 7 years

59. 24

60. 7 23¢ stamps, 1 32¢ stamp

61. 39 inches, 78 inches, and 69 inches

62. 47

63. $2\frac{1}{3}$ mph

64. 18 mph

65. 72 minutes, or 1.2 hours

66. 45 feet

67. 40 feet, 43 feet, 46 feet, and 49 feet

68. 19%

69. 300 shares of Big Brother and the Holding Company; 200 shares of Getridge Quick

70. 155 × 310 yards

71. 72 lbs.

72. $\frac{5}{3x}$

73. $420

74. Oldest, $41,000; middle, $26,000; youngest, $20,500

75. 38, 5, and 23

76. 25

77. 5 hours, 59 minutes (5.98 hours)

78. 20 minutes ($\frac{1}{3}$ hour)

79. $7\frac{1}{2}$ minutes ($\frac{1}{8}$ hour)

80. $5.60

81. 3 gallons

82. $51.50

83. 12 quarters, 7 dimes, 21 nickels

84. 8.5 years

85. 40 hours

86. (a) 227,573 (b) About 203,984

87. About 2 hours, 39 minutes (or 2.647 hours)

88. About 6 hours, 45 minutes (or 6.75 hours)

89. About 96 miles

90. 32

91. 535

92. About a mile and a half

93. About 12.6 minutes (0.2105 hour)

94. About 26.7 minutes (0.444 hour)

95. 18 feet

96. Ben 24, Ray 6

97. Matsuko 34, Kazuko 17

98. 11 years ago

99. Eve 66, Dee 33

100. 27 square feet

101. 15 meters × 4 meters

102. 110°, 55°, and 15°

103. 24 inches

104. $28,000

105. 22%

106. 2.5 quarts

107. $\frac{12}{7}$ quarts (about 1.7 quarts)

108. 11 feet and 15 feet

109. 28 $185 suits and 12 $235 suits

110. 41 volts and 24 volts

111. Airplane: 353 mph; wind: 32 mph

112. Cyclist: about 11 mph; pedestrian: about 3.5 mph

113. 1,078 lbs

114. 12 feet

115. 330

116. 31

117. 16 inches × 13 inches

118. 480 mph

119. About 33.9 amperes

120. 12,500
121. 1 second
122. 5 seconds
123. 3 inches
124. About 6.12 (or 2.5 $\sqrt{6}$) seconds
125. 35¢
126. 14 × 35
127. Two possible answers: 3.1 (3 hours 6 minutes) or .9 hours (54 minutes)
128. TV's: $579; VCR's: $359
129. 80 feet
130. 62 mph
131. 16
132. $4000
133. 68°
134. 71°
135. 4:1
136. 57.6 ounces
137. About 358
138. 32 feet
139. About 2,428
140. $5\frac{1}{7}$ hours
141. 13
142. (a) 3,176; (b) 1,750,000; (c) 30 miles
143. 4
144. 12 feet 10 inches × 3 feet 8 inches
145. 17%
146. $419.00
147. $4.83
148. 15%
149. 64 feet
150. $.076
151. 3:25 PM
152. 450 miles
153. 6 miles
154. About 9 years 4 months (112 months)
155. $1,761.99
156. $140,992.11
157. 12.14%
158. About 11.9 years
159. $P = 588{,}000e^{.010535t}$; estimate of population in 1990, 806,554 (actual population was about 935,000)
160. About 45 years
161. About 5.8 grams
162. 289 years
163. 6,600 years
164. 47
165. $59.05